THE ILLUSTRATED WILDLIFE ENCYCLOPEDIA

NATURE'S PREDATORS

This edition is published by Hermes House

Hermes House is an imprint of Anness Publishing Limited, Hermes House, 88-89 Blackfriars Road, London SE1 8HA
tel. 020 7401 2077; fax 020 7633 9499; info@anness.com

© Anness Publishing Limited 2000, 2003
1 3 5 7 9 10 8 6 4 2

Publisher: Joanna Lorenz
Managing Editor, Children's Books: Gilly Cameron Cooper
Senior Editor: Nicole Pearson
Compendium Editor: Jennifer Williams
Designers: Ann Samuel, Simon Wilder
Illustrators: David Webb, Vanessa Card, Julian Baker
Production Controller: Ann Childers
Editorial Reader: Jonathan Marshall

Previously published as four separate volumes: *Snakes*, *Birds of Prey*, *Crocodiles* and *Sharks*.

PICTURE CREDITS

b=bottom, t=top, c= centre, l= left, r= right

Thanks to the National Birds of Prey Centre in Newent for their help in creating this section.

SNAKES

Jane Burton/Warren Photographic: pages 35c, 46-47 and 54tr; Bruce Coleman Ltd: pages 12bl, 14bl, 20br, 21r, 22tl, 25tl, 24tl, 25cr, 26cl, 26tr, 26br, 27tr, 27bl, 28br, 33br, 34t, 35b, 36br, 37t, 39cr, 39bl, 39r, 40bl, 42c, 43bl, 45br, 50cl, 50br, 52bl, 52br, 54tr, 54cr, 54b, 56cr, 56b, 59tr, 60bl, 62bl, 62cr, 65br, 66tr and 67b; Ecoscene: pages 25cr and 65tl; Mary Evans Picture Library: pages 51tr and 59br; FLPA: pages 17cr, 17cl, 22c, 24bl, 29tl, 29tr, 32tl, 32c, 37cr, 38-39, 41tr, 41bl, 44cr, 45t, 45bl, 46-47, 49tr, 51cl, 51br, 54cl, 56-57, 57bl, 58b, 58r, 61tl, 63bl and 66br; Holt Studios International: pages 28tl, 52tr and 64tl; Nature Photographers: page 56bc; NHPA: pages 13bl, 14tl, 15tr, 15bl, 17tl, 20tl, 24br, 25tl, 25br, 28bl, 29bl, 29br, 37cl, 42-43, 43tr, 43cr, 44bl, 48cl, 53tl, 53cl, 53bl, 55cl, 55r, 56tl, 57t and 59c; Oxford Scientific Films: pages 12tc, 18-19, 30-31, 48t, 49b and 62br; Planet Earth Pictures: pages 34b, 40cl, 40br, 40tr, 44tr, 48br, 49c, 60tr, 60br, 61cr, 63cr, 66cl, 67tl and 67tr; Visual Arts Library: pages 11br, 17br and 33bl; Zefa Pictures: page 57br.

Special photography: Kim Taylor/Warren Photographic: pages 8-9, 10-11, 13tr, 16bl, 16bc, 17tr, 18-19, 20-21, 22cl, 22bl, 30-31, 33tr, 35t, 37bl, 40tl, 40-41, 41tr, 42bl, 53r, 58cl, 62tr, 63t, 64b, 65c, 65bl.

BIRDS OF PREY

Heather Angel: 75bl, 87bl, 116br, 119bl, 125tl. Ardea: Ake Linday: 114bl/M. Watson: 98bl. BBC Natural History Unit: Bernard Castelein: 82tl, 121b/Nick Garbutt: 78tr/Tony Heald: 85tr, 100bl/David Kjaar: 115bl/Neil P. Lucas: 126br/Klaus Nigge: 88tr, 95tr/Dietmar Nill: 75tr, 94bl/Pete Oxford: 94c/Chris Packham: 91m/Rico & Ruiz: 102bl, 107tl, 127c/Artur Tabor: 112bl/Richard du Toit: 77c, 78br/Tom Vezo: 91tl/Tom Walmsley: 89c. Bruce Coleman: Jane Burton: 108tl/Erik Bjurstrom: 122bl/John Cancalosi: 120tl/Robert P. Carr: 83tr/Jose Luis Gonzalez Grande: 77b, 112bl/Peter A. Hinchliffe: 75br/Steve Kaufman: 82br/Antonio Manzanares: 86tr, 103tr/Luiz Claudio Marigo: 99cr/George McCarthy: 96tl, 106c/Dr. Scott Nielsen: 121tr/Alan G. Potts: 71br, 109tl/Jeff Foot Productions: 85bl, 94tl/Hans Reinhard: 103c/John Shaw: 97br, 110bl/Kim Taylor: 109c/Rod Williams: 116tl/Gunter Ziesler: 73tl. Ancient Art & Architecture Collection: 90bl. Planet Earth: Frank Blackburn: 102tr/John R. Bracegirdle: 89l/Darroch Donald: 70bl/Carol Farneti-Foster: 117c/Nick Garbutt: 104tl, 104c, 104tr, 105tl, 105c, 105bl/Ken Lucas: 107tl/Andrew Mounter: 122br/Susan & Alan Parker: 72br/Johan le Roux: 111cl/Keith Scholey: 98tr/Jonathan Scott: 99tl, 101br/Anup & Manoj Shah: 120c. Ecoscene: Ian Beames: 125c/Robert Walker: 124c. Mary Evans: 71b, 79tl, 83br, 87tr, 116bl, 125bl. Oxford Scientific Films: Miriam Austerman: 99br, 126tr/Adrian Bailey: 118br/Bob Bennett: 76bl/G I Bernard: 85br, 120br/Mike Birkhead: 126bl/Tony & Liz Bomford: 107bl/David Cayless: 127bl/Susan Day: 127tl/John Downer: 119c/Carol Farneti-Foster: 79tr/David B. Fleetham: 113b/Dennis Green: 105br/Mark Hamblin: 85tl, 111cr/Mike Hill: 115tr/Tim Jackson: 89tr/Lon E. Lauber: 73c, 118tl/Michael Leach: 72tr, 115cl, 90tr/Ted Levin: 95bl, 115tr/Rob Nunnington: 78bl/Ben Osborne: 121c/Stan Osolinski: 72bl, 73br, 84b, 100tl, 101tr, 118bl/Mike Price: 117tl/Norbert Rosing: 113tr/Frank Scheidermeyer: 101bl/David Tipling: 124tl/David Thompson: 91tr/Barbara Tyack: 119tl/Konrad Wothe: 71tr, 86bl. FLPA: J J Hinojosa: 110tr. Michael Holford: 123br. Gallo Images: Anthony Bannister: 74tr, 77tl, 95tl/Nigel Dennis: 95br, 98br, 103bl, 111br, 117bl/Clem Haagner: 87c, 91bl, 106tr, 111tr, 117tr/Hein von Horsten: 101tl, 106tl/M. Philip Kahl: 99c/Peter Lillie: 109tl /Eric Reisinger: 87tl. Images Colour Library: 80-81, 92-93, 96-97, 104-105, 118-119. NHPA: Stephen Dalton: 79c/Manfred Danegger: 88b/Martin Harvey: 115br/William Paton: 89b. Papilio: 76tr, 90c. David Pike: 76bl, 97bl, 97tl, 97tr. Kim Taylor: 71tl, 75tr, 80br, 80bl, 80tl, 81bl, 81tr, 85tl, 84tl, 92tl, 92tr, 95c, 95tl, 93br. Warren Photographic: Jane Burton: 108cl, 108c, 108cr/Kim Taylor: 70-71c, 79br, 85tl, 123tl, 123tr.

CROCODILES

ABPL: 161t/C Haagner: 151c, 148b/C Hughes: 154b/M Harvey: 151tl, 144bl/R de la Harper: 162b, 163t/S Adev: 149b; Ancient Art & Architecture Collection: 168br; BBC Natural History Unit/A Shah: 151t/J Rotman: 136bl/M Barton: 134bl/P Oxford: 175br/T Pooley: 161c; Biofotos/B Rogers: 169t; Bruce Coleman/Animal Ark: 173tl/CB & DW Frith: 181br/E & P Bauer: 182b/G Cozzi: 164b/J McDonald: 173c/LC Marigo: 165bl, 167br, 172t, 175c/M Plage: 178c/R Williams: 152br, CM Dixon: 154br; ET archive: 152bl; FLPA/G Lacz: 157tl/W Wisniewski: 142b, G Webb: 143c, 185b; Heather Angel: 145cr, 186b; M & P Fogden: 140t, 147bl, 154t, 159cl, 172c, 175b, 184t, Mary Evans Picture Library: 150bl, 146br, 167bl; Natural History Museum, London: 176b, 177c; Nature Photographers Ltd/EA James: 136br/D Heuchlin: 137c, 149t, 160t, 165c, 171(both), 184b, 185tr, 185b, 187tl/E Soder: 181bl/H&V Ingen: 133bl/J Shaw: 175t/K Schafer: 153t/ M Harvey: 146bl/M Wendler: 151tr, 167c, 185cr, 187tr, 187b/N Wu: 153b/NJ Dennis: 165cl, 187c/O Rogge: 142tl/P Scott: 184c/S Robinson: 141br; Oxford Scientific Films/A Bee: 181tr/B Wright: 157tr/Breck P Kent: 185tl/E Robinson: 4tr, 30b/ER Degginger: 7cr/F Ehrenstrom: 6tr/F Schneidermeyer: 15cl/F Whitehead: 40t/J Macdonald: 9c/J McCammon: 182t /J Robinson: 146tl/K Westerkov: 178b/M Deeble & V Stone: 143tl, 145cl, 148tl, 155t, 155b, 159b, 162t, 165cr/M Fogden: 141tl/M Pitts: 174b/M Sewell: 134t/O Newman: 167t/R Davies: 169b/S Leszczynski: 141cr, 179b, 183t/S Osolinski: 152bl, 158tr, 156c, 157cl, 169c/S Turner: 175bl/W Shattil: 147t; Planet Earth/A & M Shah: 151c/B Kenney: 160b/C Farnetti: 158b/D Kjaer: 165tl/D Maitland: 166b/DA Ponton: 145b/G Bell: 149c/J Lythgoe: 158t/J Scott: 143tr, 150bl, 151b, 157bl/JA Provenza: 144tr/K Lucas: 130-131, 137bl, 170t, 179tl (both), 183cl/M & C Denis-Huot: 140cl/N Greaves: 150tl/P Stephenson: 186t/R de la Harper: 159tl, 168t, 172b; Survival Anglia/F Koster: 170b/M Linley: 180t/M Price: 168bl/V Sinha: 135t, 99cr; Twentieth Century Fox: 120b.

SHARKS

BBC Natural History Unit: A James: 209t:/D Hall: 227cl/J Rotman: 195br, 197tl, 203tl, 205tr, 207tl, 235cl, 243tl/M Dohrn: 250tl/T Krull: 230br; Bridgeman Art Library: 218br, 231tl; British Museum: 191br; Bruce Coleman/Pacific Stock: 237br; FLPA: DP Wilson: 211br, 219tr, 237cr/LS Sorisio: 215bl; Gallo Images: /G Cliff: 221tr/J Rotman: 195bl, 196bl; Heather Angel: 241cr; Innerspace Visions: A Nachoum: 194bl/B Cranston: 191tl, 203br, 204bl, 205bl, 214tl, 215br, 254tl, 243bl/B Cropp: 207cl/B Rasner: 201tr/D Fleetham: 198tr, 226tl, 256br, 244tl/D Perrine: 198bl, 199bl, 200cl, 201tl, 201bl, 202bl, 203cl, 205bl, 215c, 217bl, 225tl, 224br, 225bl, 226br, 251tr, 255br, 256tl, 240t, 247cl, 247bl, 247br/D Shen: 192tl/F Schulke: 243br/H Hall: 198ct, 218tl, 218bl/I Rutzky: 235bl/J Campbell: 245b/J Jaskolski: 241cl/J Knowlton: 216bl/J Morrissey: 221bl, 228br/J Rotman: 217br, 225tr, 235cr, 245tl/JC Carrie: 217cl/JD Watt: 190bl, 212tr, 225br/M Conlin: 217tl, 219br, 229cr, 239cl, 241tr/M Snyderman: 196br, 205tl, 205cl, 206br/M Strickland: 247tl/MP O'Neill: 220bl/MS Nolan: 207bl, 208tl/N Wu: 220tl/P Humann: 214bl/R Ellis: 235tl/R Herrmann: 204tr/R Kuiter: 192br, 228tl/R Troll: 234bl/S Drogin: 206tl/S Gonor: 229tl, 244bl/SH Gruber: 60tl/T Haight: 25bl/W Schubert: 14tl; Mary Evans Picture Library: 53cr; National Geographic: 60tl/N Calogianis: 225tl; NHPA: 195cr, 193bl, 210tl, 210bl/K Schafer: 208bl/N Wu: 209 (all), 215b, 227tl, 237cl, 245cl; Oxford Scientific Films: D Fleetham: 201br, 224cl, 237cr, 243cr/G Soury: 207br, 212bl/H Hall: 191tr, 225cr, 252 (all), 255tl/K Gowlett: 197tr/M Deeble & V Stone: 222, 223bl/M Gibson: 242bl/N Wu: 192bl/R Herrmann: 206bl, 239tl/R Kuiter: 228cl/W Wu: 233tr, 241b; Papilio Photographic: 202tl, 239bl; Planet Earth: D Perrine: 222br, 225br/G Bell: 193l, 196tl/G Douwma: 208br/J Seagrim: 219tl/J&A Moran: 245cr/K Amsler: 240b/K Lucas: 235cl, 258tl/M Snyderman: 191bl, 195tr, 215tl, 253bc/N Wu: 195tr, 197br/P Atkinson: 199tr; Scott Mycock & Rachel Cavanagh: 251tr; Seitre Bios: 194br; South American Pictures: R Francis: 231bl; Universal Pictures: 242tr; Zefa/M Jozon: 213tl.

THE ILLUSTRATED WILDLIFE ENCYCLOPEDIA

NATURE'S
PREDATORS

HERMES
HOUSE

CONTENTS

INTRODUCING PREDATORS.....6

SNAKES.....8

BIRDS OF PREY.....68

CROCODILES.....128

SHARKS......188

Introducing Predators

From the great white shark and the saltwater crocodile to the king cobra and the golden eagle, this book is packed with information about some of the world's most spectacular predators. It explains how their supreme skill as hunters depends on their keen senses, and weapons such as razor-sharp teeth, fearsome talons and poisonous fangs.

Take an in-depth look at every aspect of their biology and ecology – how their bodies work, how they feed, where they live and how they defend themselves. Find out how we can conserve these fascinating animals whose future is threatened by habitat destruction, pollution and trade in their skins, fins and other body parts. This book powerfully conveys the wild beauty of these predators, whose future rests in our hands.

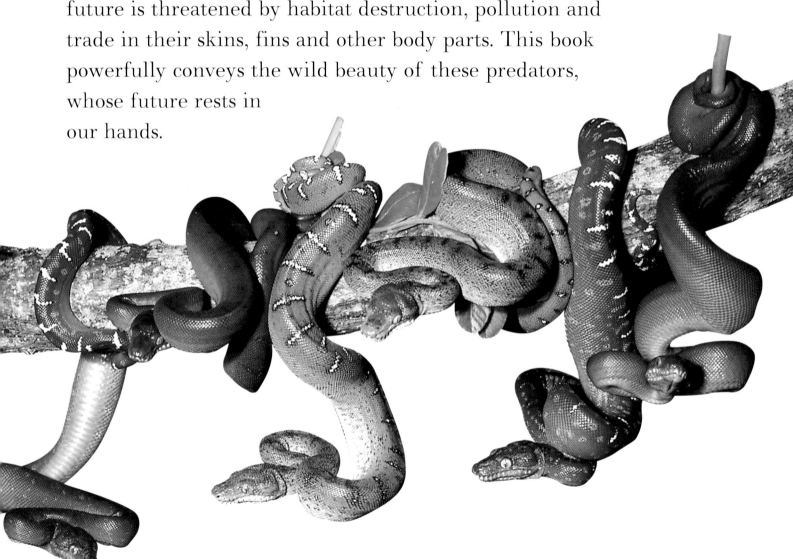

FOOD CHAINS AND WEBS

A simple food chain starts with plants that utilize the Sun's energy to build new tissues. Plants are consumed by plant-eaters (herbivores), plant-eaters in turn are devoured by meat-eaters (carnivores), and meat-eaters are caught by even more powerful meat-eaters. At the top of this chain of life are predators, such as snakes, eagles, crocodiles and sharks.

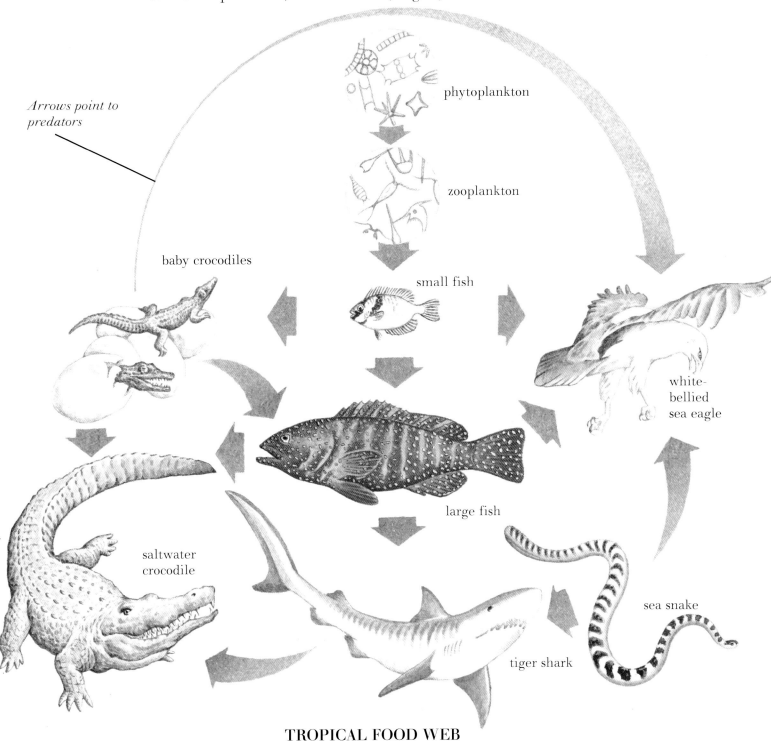

Arrows point to predators

phytoplankton

zooplankton

baby crocodiles

small fish

white-bellied sea eagle

saltwater crocodile

large fish

tiger shark

sea snake

TROPICAL FOOD WEB

This simplified food web shows the feeding connections between a community of animals in tropical inshore waters in the western Pacific. Here, top predators include tiger sharks, saltwater crocodiles, sea snakes and white-bellied sea eagles.

7

SNAKES

Snakes are among the most feared and least understood of all predators. They vary in size from the tiny blind snake that can fit into the palm of your hand to the enormous Burmese python. Some snakes kill their victims by squeezing them to death in seconds, others swallow their live prey whole.

Author: Barbara Taylor
Consultant: Michael Chinery

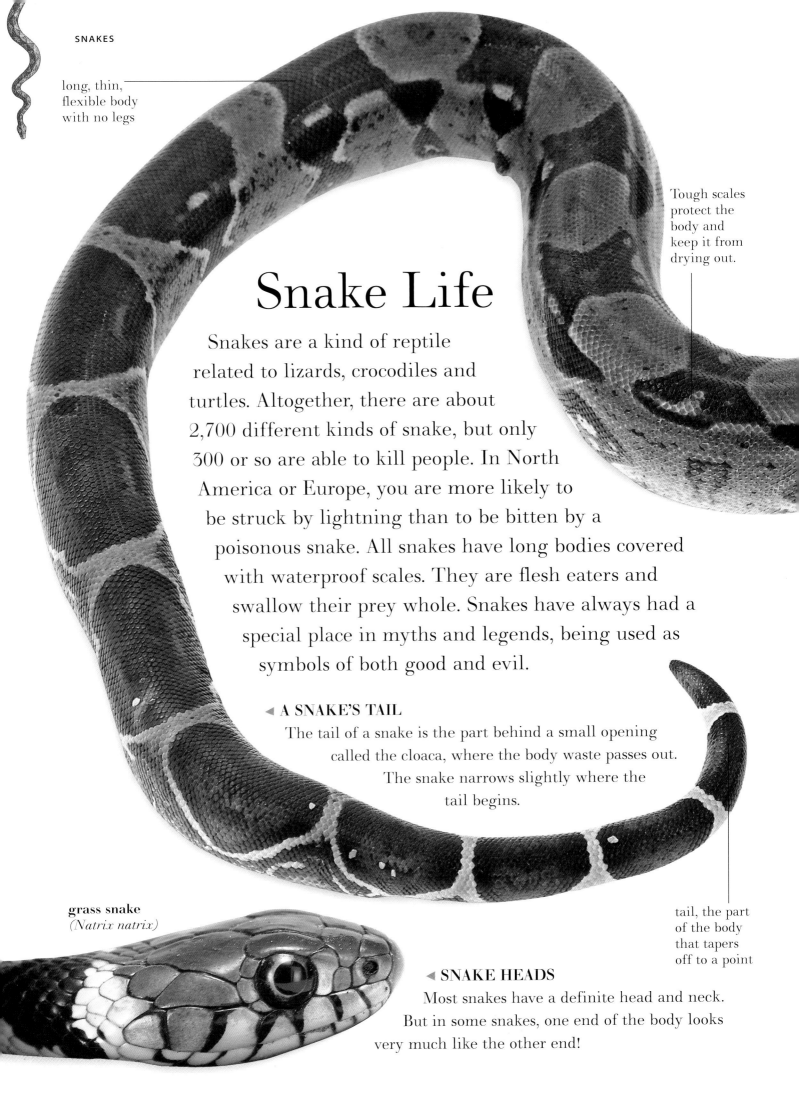

long, thin, flexible body with no legs

Tough scales protect the body and keep it from drying out.

Snake Life

Snakes are a kind of reptile related to lizards, crocodiles and turtles. Altogether, there are about 2,700 different kinds of snake, but only 300 or so are able to kill people. In North America or Europe, you are more likely to be struck by lightning than to be bitten by a poisonous snake. All snakes have long bodies covered with waterproof scales. They are flesh eaters and swallow their prey whole. Snakes have always had a special place in myths and legends, being used as symbols of both good and evil.

◄ **A SNAKE'S TAIL**

The tail of a snake is the part behind a small opening called the cloaca, where the body waste passes out. The snake narrows slightly where the tail begins.

grass snake
(Natrix natrix)

tail, the part of the body that tapers off to a point

◄ **SNAKE HEADS**

Most snakes have a definite head and neck. But in some snakes, one end of the body looks very much like the other end!

◀ **FORKED TONGUES**

Snakes and some lizards have forked tongues. A snake flicks its tongue to taste and smell the air. This gives the snake a picture of what is around it. A snake does this every few seconds if it is hunting or if there is any danger nearby.

rattlesnake
(Crotalus)

Colombian rainbow boa
(Epicrates cenchria maurus)

▲ **SCALY ARMOR**

A covering of tough, dry scales grows out of a snake's skin. The scales usually hide the skin. After a big meal, the scaly skin stretches so that the skin becomes visible between the scales. A snake's scales protect its body while allowing it to stretch, coil and bend. The scales may be either rough or smooth.

red-tailed boa
(Boa constrictor)

Did you know? Snakes never feel slimy to the touch.

Did you know? A boa squeezes its prey to death in its coils.

eye has no eyelid

forked tongue

Medusa

An ancient Greek myth tells of Medusa, a monster with snakes for hair. Anyone who looked at her was turned to stone. Perseus managed to avoid this fate by using his polished shield to look only at the monster's reflection. He cut off Medusa's head and carried it home, dripping with blood. As each drop touched the earth, it turned into a snake.

Shapes and Sizes

Can you imagine a snake as tall as a three-storey house? The reticulated python is this big. The biggest snakes' bodies measure nearly a metre round. Other snakes are as thin as a pencil and small enough to fit into the palm of your hand. Snakes also have different shapes to suit their environments. Sea snakes, for example, have flat bodies and tails like oars to help them push against the water and move forwards.

▼ **THICK AND THIN**

Vipers mostly have thick bodies with much thinner, short tails. The bags of poison on either side of a viper's head take up a lot of space, so the head is quite large.

rhinoceros viper
(*Bitis nasicornis*)

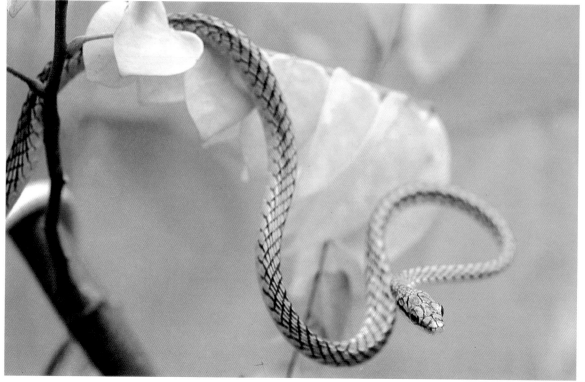

◄ **LONG AND THIN**

A tree snake's long, thin shape helps it slide along leaves and branches. Even its head is long, pointed and very light so that it does not weigh the snake down as it reaches for the next branch.

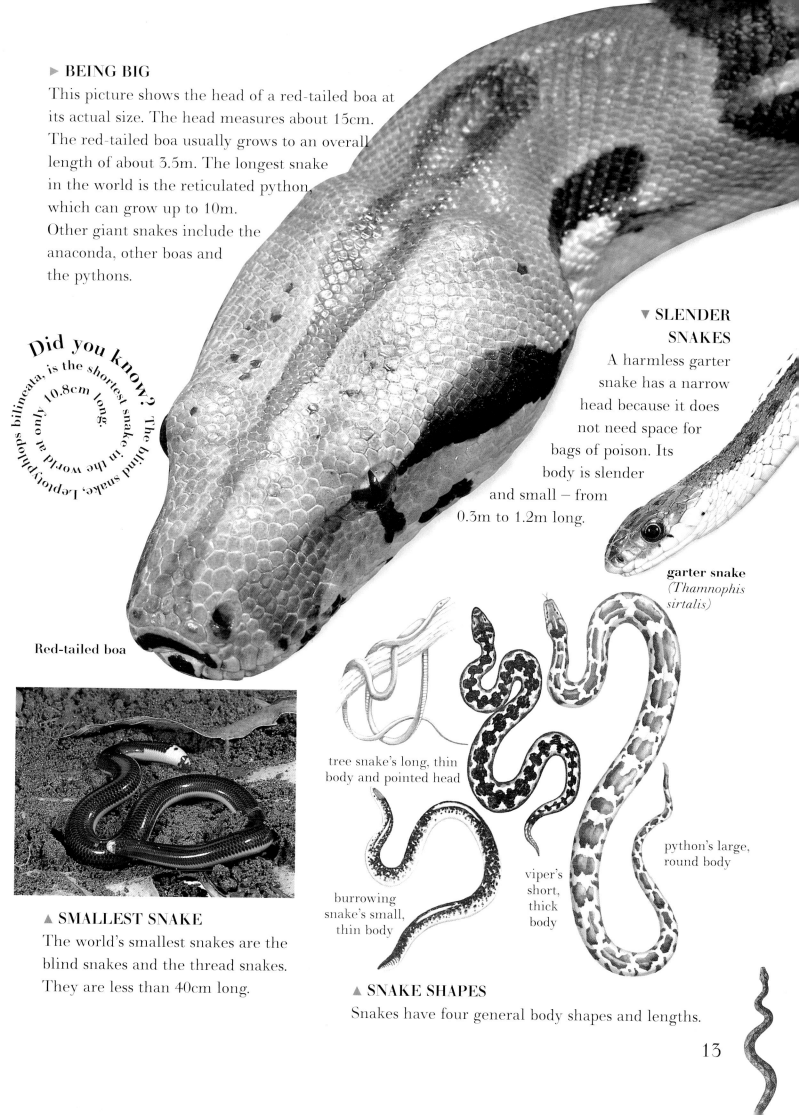

▶ BEING BIG

This picture shows the head of a red-tailed boa at its actual size. The head measures about 15cm. The red-tailed boa usually grows to an overall length of about 3.5m. The longest snake in the world is the reticulated python, which can grow up to 10m. Other giant snakes include the anaconda, other boas and the pythons.

Did you know? The blind snake, Leptotyphlops bilineata, is the shortest snake in the world at only 10.8cm long.

Red-tailed boa

▼ SLENDER SNAKES

A harmless garter snake has a narrow head because it does not need space for bags of poison. Its body is slender and small – from 0.3m to 1.2m long.

garter snake
(Thamnophis sirtalis)

tree snake's long, thin body and pointed head

burrowing snake's small, thin body

viper's short, thick body

python's large, round body

▲ SMALLEST SNAKE

The world's smallest snakes are the blind snakes and the thread snakes. They are less than 40cm long.

▲ SNAKE SHAPES

Snakes have four general body shapes and lengths.

13

egg-eating snake
(Dasypeltis fasciata)

◀ **STRETCHY STOMACH**
Luckily, the throat and gut of the egg-eating snake are so elastic that its thin body can stretch enough to swallow a whole egg. Muscles in the throat and first part of the gut help force food down into the stomach.

How Snakes Work

A snake has a stretched-out inside to match its long, thin outside. The backbone extends along the whole body with hundreds of ribs joined to it. There is not much room for organs such as the heart, lungs, kidneys and liver, so these organs are thin shapes to fit inside the snake's body. Many snakes have only one lung. The stomach and gut are stretchy so that they can hold large meals. When a snake swallows big prey, it pushes the opening of the windpipe up from the floor of the mouth in order to keep breathing. Snakes are cold-blooded, which means that their body temperature is the same as their surroundings.

right lung is very long and thin and does the work of two lungs

liver is very long and thin

flexible tail bone, which extends from the back bone

▼ **INSIDE A SNAKE**
This diagram shows the inside of a male snake. The organs are arranged to fit the snake's long shape. In most species, paired organs, such as the kidneys, are the same size and placed opposite each other.

▲ **COLD-BLOODED CREATURE**
Like all snakes, the banded rattlesnake is cold-blooded.

rectum through which waste is passed to the cloaca

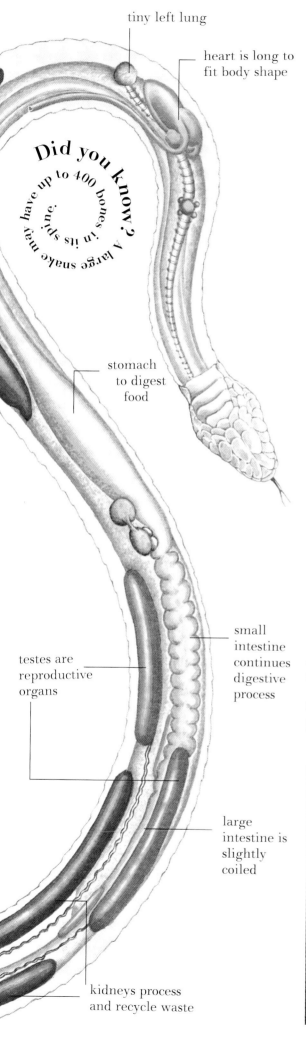

tiny left lung

heart is long to fit body shape

Did you know? A large snake may have up to 400 bones in its spine.

stomach to digest food

testes are reproductive organs

small intestine continues digestive process

large intestine is slightly coiled

kidneys process and recycle waste

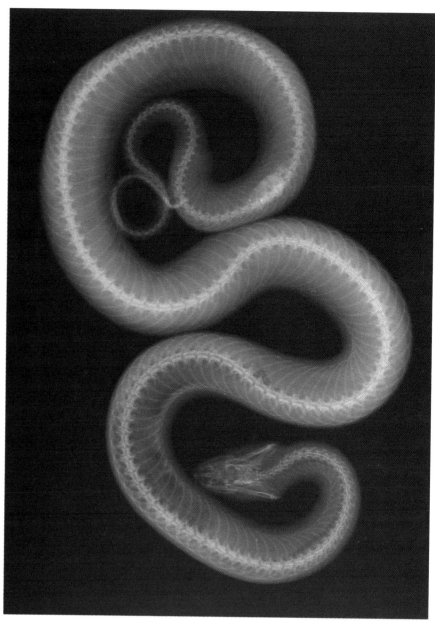

▲ SNAKE BONES

This X-ray of a grass snake shows the delicate bones that make up its skeleton. There are no arm, leg, shoulder or hip bones. The snake's ribs do not extend into the tail.

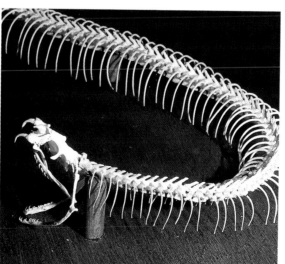

◄ SKELETON

A snake's skeleton is made up of a skull and a backbone with ribs arching out from it. The free ends of the ribs are linked by muscles.

15

Scaly Skin

▼ **HORNED SNAKE**

As its name suggests, the European nose-horned viper has a strange horn on its nose. The horn is made up of small scales that lie over a bony or fleshy lump sticking out at the end of the nose.

A snake's scales are extra-thick pieces of skin. Like a suit of armor, the scales protect the snake from bumps and scrapes as it moves. They also allow the skin to stretch when the snake moves or eats. Scales are usually made of a horny substance called keratin. Every part of a snake's body is covered by a layer of scales, including the eyes. The clear, bubble-like scale that protects each eye is called a brille or spectacle.

nose-horned viper
(Vipera ammodytes)

▼ **SCUTES**

Most snakes have a row of broad scales, called scutes, underneath their bodies. The scutes go across a snake's body from side to side, and end where the tail starts. Scutes help snakes to grip the ground.

▼ **WARNING RATTLE**

The rattlesnake has a number of hollow tail-tips that make a buzzing sound when shaken. The snake uses this sound to warn enemies. When it sheds its skin, a section at the end of the tail is left, adding another piece to the rattle.

rattlesnake's rattle

corn snake's scutes

16

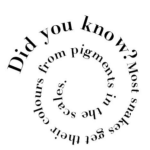

▶ SKIN SCALES

The scales of a snake grow out of the top layer of the skin, called the epidermis. There are different kinds of scales. Keeled scales may help snakes to grip surfaces, or break up a snake's outline for camouflage. Smooth scales make it easier for the snake to squeeze through tight spaces.

Look closely at the rough scales of the puff adder (left) and you will see a raised ridge, or keel, sticking up in the middle of each one.

Did you know? *Most snakes get their colours from pigments in the scales.*

corn snake's scale

The wart snake (right) uses its scales to grip its food. Its rough scales help the snake to keep a firm hold on slippery fish until it can swallow them. The snake's scales do not overlap.

Eternal Youth

A poem written in the Middle East about 3,700 years ago tells a story about why snakes can shed their skins. The hero of the poem is Gilgamesh (shown here holding a captured lion). He finds a magic plant that will make a person young again. While he is washing at a pool, a snake eats the plant. Since then, snakes have been able to shed their skins and become young again. But people have never found the plant — which is why they always grow old and die.

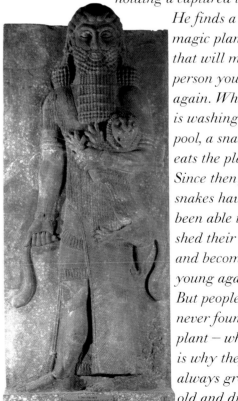

The green scales and stretched blue skin (left) belong to a boa. These smooth scales help the boa to slide over leafy branches. Burrowing snakes have smooth scales so that they can slip through soil.

Did you know? *The hairy bush viper has pointed scales with curled tips, making it look hairy.*

1 In the days before its skin peels, a snake is sluggish and its colours become dull. Its eyes turn cloudy as their coverings loosen. About a day before moulting, the eyes clear.

Focus on New Skin

About six times a year, an adult snake wriggles out of its old, tight skin to reveal a new, shiny skin underneath. Snakes shed their worn-out skin and scales in one piece. This process is called moulting or sloughing. Snakes only moult when a new layer of skin and scales has grown underneath the old skin.

2 The paper-thin layer of outer skin and scales first starts to peel away around the mouth. The snake rubs its jaws and chin against rocks or rough bark, and crawls through plants. This helps to push off the loose layer of skin.

Did you know? A baby snake may shed its skin when it is only a few days old.

3 The outer layer of skin gradually peels back from the head over the rest of the body. The snake slides out of its old skin, which comes off inside-out. It is rather like taking hold of a long sock at the top and peeling it down over your leg and foot!

Did you know? Female snakes often shed their skin just before giving birth.

4 A snake usually takes several hours to shed its whole skin. The old skin is moist and supple soon after shedding, but gradually dries out to become crinkly and rather brittle. The moulted skin is a copy of the snake's scale pattern. It is very delicate, and if you hold it up to the light, it is almost see-through.

5 A shed skin is longer than the snake itself. This is because the skin stretches as the snake wriggles free.

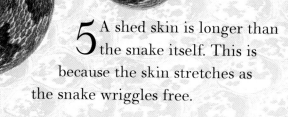

19

Snakes on the Move

A person can walk faster than a snake can move

corn snake
(Elaphe guttata)

For animals without legs, snakes move around very well. They can glide over or under the ground, climb trees and swim through water. A few snakes can even parachute through the air. Snakes are not speedy – most move at about 3kph. Their bendy backbones give them a wavy movement. They push themselves along using muscles joined to their ribs. The scales on their skin also grip surfaces to help with movement.

▶ S-SHAPED MOVER

Most snakes move in an S-shaped path, pushing the side curves of their bodies backwards against the surface they are travelling on or through. The muscular waves of the snake's body hit surrounding objects and the whole body is pushed forward from there.

▲ SWIMMING SNAKE

The banded sea snake's stripes stand out as it glides through the water. Snakes swim using S-shaped movements. A sea snake's tail is flattened from side to side to give it extra power, like the oar on a row boat.

▼ CONCERTINA SNAKE

The green whip snake moves with an action rather like a concertina. The concertina is played by squeezing it forwards and backwards.

20

▶ SIDEWINDING

The way snakes that live on loose sand move along is called sidewinding. The snake anchors its head and tail in the sand and throws the middle part of its body sideways.

Did you know? The fastest land snake is the black mamba, moving at up to 11 kph.

▼ HOW SNAKES MOVE

Most land snakes move in four different ways, depending on the type of terrain they are crossing and the type of snake.

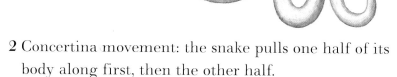

1 S-shaped movement: the snake wriggles from side to side.

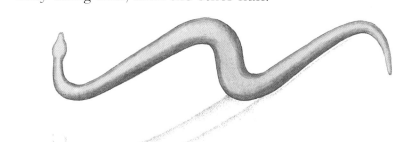

2 Concertina movement: the snake pulls one half of its body along first, then the other half.

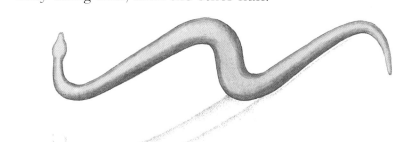

3 Sidewinding movement: the snake throws the middle part of its body forwards, keeping the head and tail on the ground.

4 Caterpillar movement: the snake uses its belly scutes to pull itself along in a straight line.

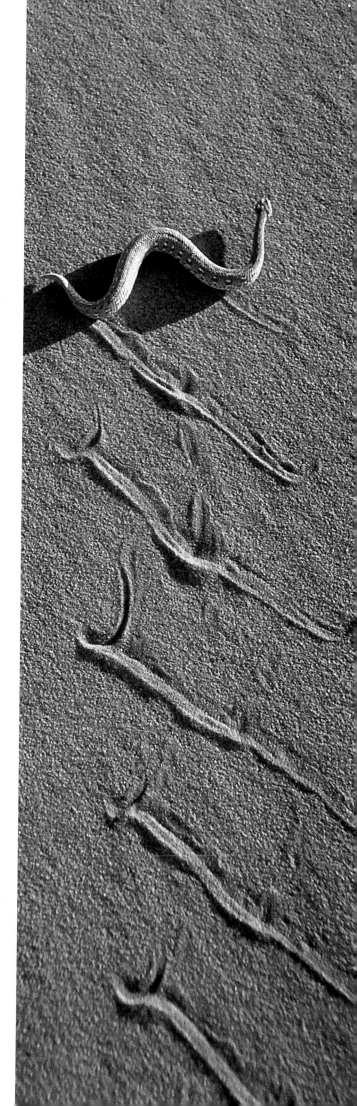

▲ EYESIGHT

Snakes have no eyelids to cover their eyes. The snakes with the best eyesight are tree snakes, such as this green mamba, and day hunters.

Snake Senses

To find prey and avoid enemies, snakes rely more on their senses of smell, taste and touch than on sight and hearing. Snakes have no ears, but they do have one earbone joined at the jaw. The lower jaw picks up sound vibrations travelling through the ground. As well as ordinary senses, snakes also have some special ones. They are one of the few animals that taste and smell with their tongues.

▲ NIGHT HUNTER

The horned viper's eyes open wide at night (*above*). During the day, its pupils close to narrow slits (*below*).

heat pits

▲ SENSING HEAT

The green tree python senses heat given off by its prey through pits on the sides of its face.

◄ THE FORKED TONGUE

When a snake investigates its surroundings, it flicks its tongue to taste the air. The forked tongue picks up tiny chemical particles of scent.

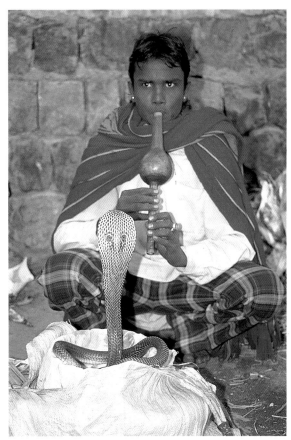

▲ HEARING

As it has no ears, the cobra cannot hear the music played by the snake charmer. It follows the movements of the pipe, which resemble a snake, and rises up as it prepares to defend itself.

► JACOBSON'S ORGAN

As a snake draws its tongue back into its mouth, it presses the forked tip into the two openings of the Jacobson's organ. This organ is in the roof of the mouth and it analyzes tastes and smells.

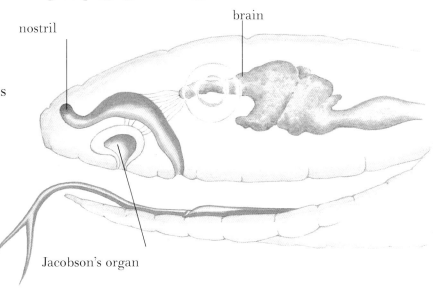

nostril

brain

Jacobson's organ

23

Food and Hunting

Snakes eat different foods and hunt in different ways depending on their size, their species and where they live. Some snakes eat a wide variety of food, while others have a more specialized diet. A snake has to make the most of each meal because it moves fairly slowly and does not get the chance to catch prey very often. A snake's body works at a slow rate so it can go for months without eating.

▲ **TREE HUNTERS**
A rat snake grasps a baby bluebird in its jaws and begins the process of digestion. Rat snakes often slither up trees in search of baby birds, eggs or squirrels.

rat snake
(Elaphe)

▲ **FISHY FOOD**
The tentacled snake lives on fish. It probably hides among plants, in the water and grabs fish as they swim past.

▼ **TRICKY LURE**
The Australasian death adder's colourful tail tip looks like a worm. The adder wriggles the 'worm' to lure lizards, birds and small mammals to come within its range.

◄ **EGG-EATERS**
The African egg-eater snake checks an egg with its tongue to make sure it is fresh. Then it swallows the egg whole. It uses the pointed ends of the bones in its backbone to crack the eggshell. It eats the egg and coughs up the crushed shell.

► **SURPRISE ATTACK**
Lunch for this gaboon viper is a mouse! The gaboon viper hides among dry leaves on the forest floor. Its colouring and markings make it very difficult to spot. It waits for a small animal to pass by, then grabs hold of its prey in a surprise attack. Many other snakes that hunt by day also ambush their prey.

Did you know? Sometimes a snake coughs up its prey – alive!

smooth snake
(Coronella austriaca)

◄ **SNAKE EATS SNAKE**
This smooth snake is eating an asp viper. The viper fits neatly inside the body of the smooth snake. This makes it easier to swallow than animals that are different shapes.

Teeth and Jaws

Most snakes have short, sharp teeth that are good for gripping and holding prey, but not for chewing it into smaller pieces. The teeth are not very strong, and often get broken, so they are continually being replaced. Poisonous snakes also have some larger teeth called fangs. When the snake bites, poison flows down the fangs to paralyze the prey and break down its body. All snakes swallow their prey head-first and whole.

▼ BACK FANGS

A few poisonous snakes have fangs at the back of their mouths. This African boomslang is digging its fangs hard into a chameleon's flesh to get enough poison inside.

▲ OPEN WIDE

An eyelash viper opens its mouth as wide as possible to scare an enemy. Its fangs are folded back against the roof of the mouth. When it attacks, the fangs swing forward.

viper skull

movable fangs

▲ FOLDING FANGS

Vipers and elapid snakes have fangs at the front of their mouths. A viper's long fangs can fold back. When it strikes, the fangs swing forward to stick out in front of the mouth.

26

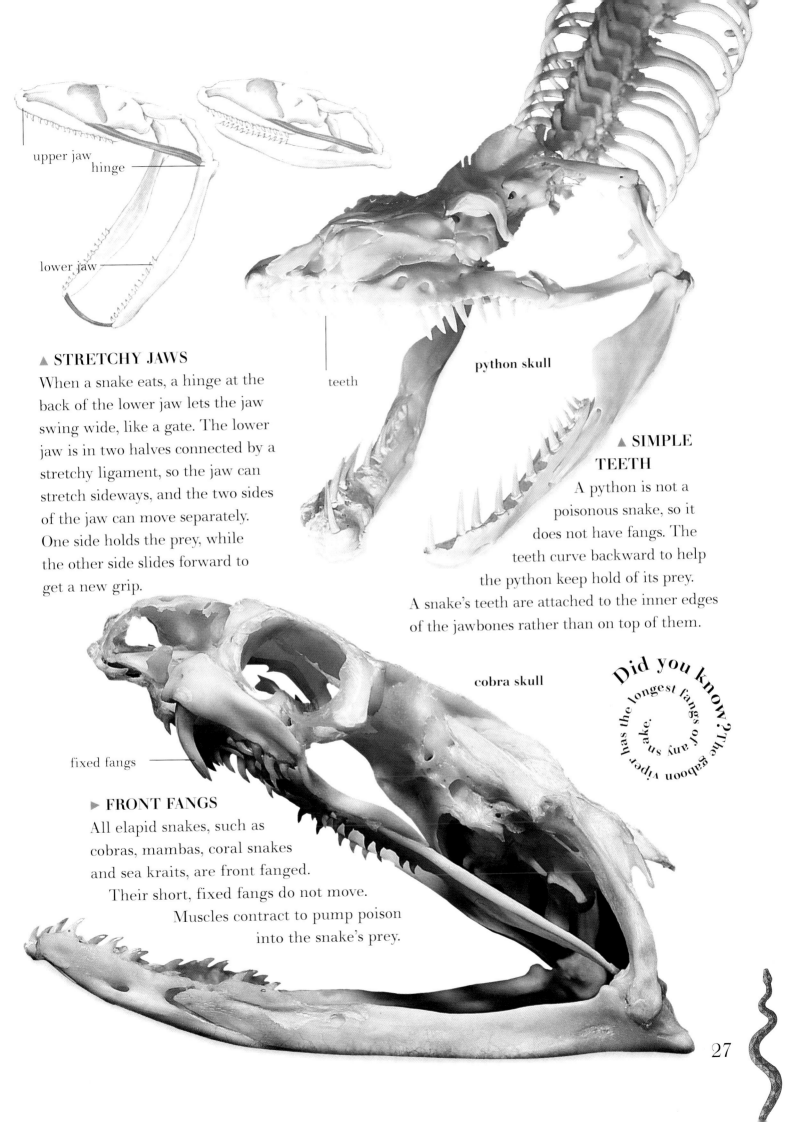

upper jaw

hinge

lower jaw

▲ STRETCHY JAWS

When a snake eats, a hinge at the back of the lower jaw lets the jaw swing wide, like a gate. The lower jaw is in two halves connected by a stretchy ligament, so the jaw can stretch sideways, and the two sides of the jaw can move separately. One side holds the prey, while the other side slides forward to get a new grip.

teeth

python skull

▲ SIMPLE TEETH

A python is not a poisonous snake, so it does not have fangs. The teeth curve backward to help the python keep hold of its prey. A snake's teeth are attached to the inner edges of the jawbones rather than on top of them.

cobra skull

fixed fangs

▶ FRONT FANGS

All elapid snakes, such as cobras, mambas, coral snakes and sea kraits, are front fanged. Their short, fixed fangs do not move. Muscles contract to pump poison into the snake's prey.

Did you know? The gaboon viper has the longest fangs of any snake.

27

American racer
(Coluber constrictor)

Stranglers and Poisoners

Most snakes kill their prey before eating it. Snakes kill by using poison or by squeezing their prey to death. Snakes that squeeze, called constrictors, stop their prey from breathing. Victims die from suffocation or shock. To swallow living or dead prey, a snake opens its jaws wide. Lots of slimy saliva helps the meal to slide down. After eating, a snake yawns widely to put its jaws back into place. Digestion can take several days, or even weeks.

▲ BIG MOUTHFUL

This American racer is trying to swallow a living frog. The frog has puffed up its body with air to make it more difficult for the snake to swallow.

▲ AT FULL STRETCH

This fer-de-lance snake is at full stretch to swallow its huge meal. It is a large pit viper that kills with poison.

▲ SWALLOWING A MEAL

The copperhead, a poisonous snake from North America, holds on to a dead mouse.

▲ KILLING TIME

A crocodile is slowly squeezed to death by a rock python. The time it takes for a constricting snake to kill its prey depends on the size of the prey and how strong it is.

► COILED KILLER

The spotted python sinks its teeth into its victim. It throws coils around the victim's body, and tightens its grip until the animal cannot breathe.

spotted python
(Liasis maculosus)

▲ HEAD-FIRST

A whiptail wallaby's legs disappear inside a carpet python's body. Snakes usually try to swallow their prey head-first so that legs, wings or scales fold back. This helps the victim to slide into the snake's stomach more easily.

▼ BREATHING TUBE

An African python shows its breathing tube. As the snake eats, the windpipe moves to the front of the mouth so that air can get to and from the lungs.

1 Rat snakes feed on rats, mice, voles, lizards, birds and eggs. Many of them hunt at night. They are good climbers and can even go up trees with smooth bark and no branches. Rat snakes find their prey by following a scent trail or waiting to ambush an animal.

Focus on Lunch

This rat snake is using its strong coils to kill a vole. Rodents, such as voles and rats, are a rat snake's favourite food. With the vole held tightly in its teeth, the snake coils around its body. It squeezes hard to stop the vole breathing. When the vole is dead, the rat snake swallows its meal head-first.

2 When the rat snake is near enough to its prey, it strikes quickly. Its sharp teeth sink into the victim's body to stop it running or flying away. The snake then loops its coils around the victim as fast as possible, before the animal can bite or scratch to defend itself.

3 Each time the vole breathes out, the rat snake squeezes harder around its rib cage to stop the vole breathing in again. Breathing becomes more difficult and soon the victim dies from suffocation.

30

4 Once the victim is dead, the rat snake loosens its coils and begins the process of swallowing. It unhinges its jaws and "walks" its mouth over its meal. The loose lower jaw stretches sideways to fit around the shape of the dead prey.

5 The rat snake swallows its meal head-first. As the vole moves down the snake's throat, its legs fold back against the sides of its body. The way the fur lies makes the vole easier to swallow. The snake's skin stretches as the meal moves down its body.

6 As the vole moves further down inside the snake's body, the skin stretches more. The ribs move apart at the front to make space for the vole's body. The snake pushes its windpipe to the front of its mouth, so that it can use it like a snorkel for breathing. It may take only one or two gulps for a snake to swallow a small animal whole.

Poisonous Snakes

Only about 700 species of snake are poisonous. Snake poison, called venom, is useful for snakes because it allows them to kill without having to fight a long battle against their prey. Some snake venom works on the prey's body, softening it and making it easier to digest. There are two main kinds of venom. One type attacks the blood and muscles. The other attacks the nervous system, stopping the heart and lungs from working.

▲ POISONOUS BITE

A copperhead gets ready to strike. Poisonous snakes use their sharp fangs to inject a lethal cocktail of chemicals into their prey. The death of victims often occurs in seconds or minutes, depending on the size of prey and where it was bitten.

▼ WARNING COLOURS

The colourful stripes of coral snakes warn predators that they are very poisonous. There are more than 50 species of coral snake, all with similar patterns. But predators remember the basic pattern and avoid all coral snakes.

spitting cobra
*(Hemachatus
haemachatus)*

▲ VENOM SPIT

Spitting cobras have an opening in their fangs to squirt venom into an enemy's face. They aim at the eyes, and the venom can cause blindness.

coral snake
(Micruroides euryxanthus)

Did you know? The most poisonous snake in the world is the black-headed sea snake.

▲ FANGS FORWARD

The copperhead is a viper, so its fangs swing down from the roof of the mouth, ready to stab its prey. The muscles around the venom glands squeeze poison through the fangs.

copperhead
*(Agkistrodon
contortrix)*

Bible Snake

At the beginning of the Bible, a snake is the cause of problems in the Garden of Eden. God told Adam and Eve never to eat fruit from the tree of knowledge of good and evil. However, the snake persuaded Eve to eat the fruit. It told Eve that the fruit would make her as clever as God. Eve gave some fruit to Adam too. As a punishment, Adam and Eve had to leave the Garden of Eden and lose the gift of eternal life.

▲ MILKING VENOM
Venom is collected from a black mamba.

green bush viper
(*Atheris squamigera*)

Focus on Vipers

Vipers are the most efficient poisonous snakes of all. Their long fangs can inject venom deep into a victim. The venom acts mainly on the blood and muscles of the prey. Vipers usually have short, thick bodies and triangular heads covered with small, ridged scales. There are two main groups of vipers. Pit vipers have large heat pits on the face, and other vipers do not.

TREE VIPER

The green bush viper lives in tropical forests, mainly in the trees. Its colouring means that it is well camouflaged against the green leaves. It lies in wait for its prey and then kills it with a quick bite. Once the prey has been caught, the snake must hold tight to stop it falling out of the tree.

BALLOON SNAKE

When threatened, the puff adder swells up like a long balloon. It does this by taking a lot of air into its lungs. Being larger makes it look even more dangerous. Puff adders also hiss loudly.

puff adder
(*Bitis arietans*)

34

rattlesnake
(Crotalus)

QUICK JAB

This rattlesnake is exploring its surroundings with its forked tongue. When the rattlesnake strikes at its prey, the hinged fangs swing forward and lock into place. The viper gives its prey a quick injection of venom, then lets go. The prey soon dies, so there is no need for the snake to hold on to it.

HEAT DETECTORS

This Sumatran pit viper has a large heat pit on each side of its head, between the nostril and the eye. The heat pit is larger than the nostril. It can detect the heat given off by warm-blooded prey. By turning its head from side to side, a pit viper can figure out the direction of its prey.

Sumatran pit viper
(Trimeresurus sumatranus)

SLOW SNAKE

Asp vipers are slow-moving snakes. They are active both by day and by night. Their main sources of food are mice, lizards and baby birds.

35

Defence

The predators of snakes include birds of prey, foxes, racoons, mongooses, baboons, crocodiles, frogs and even other snakes. If they are in danger, snakes usually prefer to hide or escape. Many come out to hunt at night, when it is more difficult for predators to catch them. If they cannot escape, snakes often make themselves look big and fierce, hiss loudly or strike at their enemies. Some pretend to be dead. Giving off a horrible smell is another good way of getting rid of an enemy!

▼ SMELLY SNAKE

The cottonmouth is named after the white colour of the inside of its mouth, which it opens to threaten enemies. If it is attacked, it can also give off a strong-smelling liquid from near the tail.

◄ EAGLE ENEMY

The short-toed eagle uses its powerful toes to catch snakes. It eats large snakes on the ground. It carries small snakes back to the nest to feed its chicks.

vine snake
(Oxybelis fulgidus)

◄ SCARY MOUTH

Like many snakes, this vine snake opens its mouth very wide to startle predators. The inside of the mouth is a bright red colour that warns off the predator. If the predator does not go away, the snake will give a poisonous bite with the fangs at the back of the mouth.

▶ PLAYING DEAD

This grass snake knows that most predators prefer healthy, living prey. So it protects itself by pretending to be dead. It rolls on to its back, opens its mouth and keeps quite still.

cottonmouth
(Agkistrodon piscivorus)

◀ DRAMATIC DISPLAY

The hognose snake is harmless, but can make itself look dangerous. It flattens its neck to make a hood. It hisses loudly and strikes towards the enemy. Then it smears itself with smelly scent.

▶ HIDDEN SNAKE

The horned viper buries itelf so that it cannot be seen by its enemies.

▲ LOOKING LARGER

The cobra spreads its hood wide to make itself look too big to swallow.

37

Did you know? In some cultures cobra venom is used as a pain reliever.

HOOD VARIETY

Like spitting cobras, the king cobra and the water cobra, this Egyptian cobra has a narrow hood. The Indian cobra and the Cape cobra of Southern Africa have much wider hoods. The Egyptian cobra ranges over much of Africa and into Arabia.

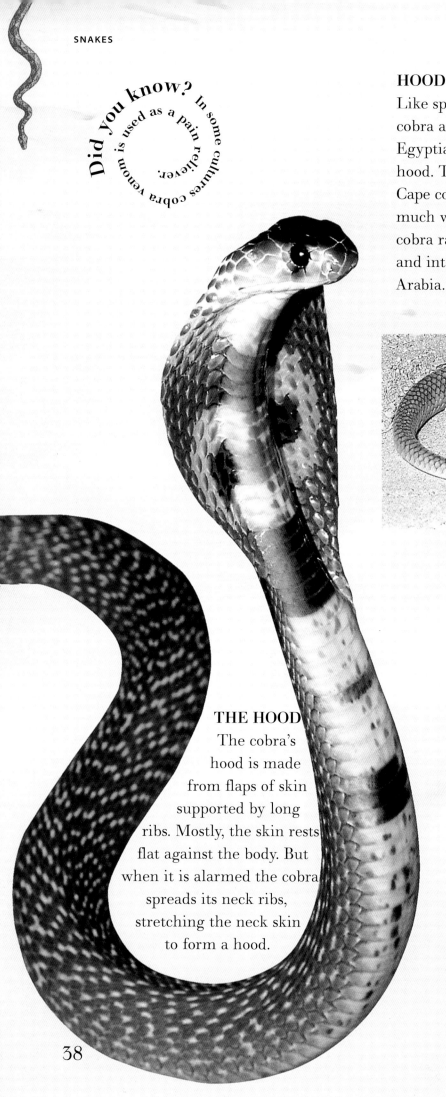

HOOD PATTERNS

Some cobras have eyespots on the back of their hoods to make them look more scary.

THE HOOD

The cobra's hood is made from flaps of skin supported by long ribs. Mostly, the skin rests flat against the body. But when it is alarmed the cobra spreads its neck ribs, stretching the neck skin to form a hood.

Focus on the Cobra and its Relatives

Cobras are very poisonous snakes. Some of them can squirt deadly venom at their enemies. Cobra venom works mainly on the nervous system, causing breathing or heart problems. Cobras are members of the elapid snake family, which includes the African mambas, the coral snakes of the Americas and all the poisonous snakes of Australia.

LARGE COBRA

The king cobra is the largest venomous snake, growing to a length of 5.5m. King cobras are the only snakes known to build a nest. The female guards her eggs and hatchlings until they leave the nest.

MIND THE MAMBA

The green mamba lives in trees. Other mambas, such as the black mamba, live mostly on the ground. Mambas are slim, long snakes that can grow up to 4m long. Their venom is very powerful and can kill a person in only ten minutes!

DO NOT DISTURB!

The Australian mainland tiger snake is a member of the elapid snake family. It is the world's fourth most poisonous snake. If it is disturbed, it puffs up its body, flattens its neck and hisses loudly. The diet of these snakes includes fish, frogs, birds and small mammals.

rainbow boa
(Epicrates cenchria)

◄ CHANGING COLOURS
The rainbow boa is iridescently coloured. Light is made up of all the colours of the rainbow. When light hits the thin outer layer of the snake's scales, it splits into different colours. The colours we see depend on the type of scales and the way light bounces off them.

Colour and Camouflage

The colours of snakes come from the pigments in the scales and from the way light reflects off the scales. Dull colours help to camouflage a snake and hide it from its enemies. Bright colours startle predators or warn them that a snake is poisonous. Harmless snakes sometimes copy the warning colours of poisonous snakes. Dark colours may help snakes to absorb heat during cooler weather. Young snakes are sometimes a different colour from their parents, but no one knows why.

milk snake
(Lampropeltis doliata)

ring-necked snake
(Diadophis punctatus)

Did you know? Milk snakes always have black bands between the red and yellow – coral snakes have the red and yellow touching.

◄ **BRIGHT COLOURS**
This snake's red tail draws attention away from the most vital part of its body – the head.

◀ COLOUR COPIES

The bright red, yellow and
black bands of this milk snake copy
the colouring of the poisonous coral
snake. The milk snake is not poisonous, but
predators leave it alone – just in case! This
colouring is found in milk snakes
in the southeast of the USA.

▼ NO COLOUR

White snakes, with no colour at all,
are called albinos. In the wild, these
snakes stand out against background
colours and are usually killed by
predators before they can reproduce.

▼ SNAKE MARKINGS

Many snakes are marked with
colourful patches. These markings are
usually caused
by groups of
different
pigments in
the scales.

red-tailed boa
(Boa constrictor)

◀ CLEVER CAMOUFLAGE

Among the dead leaves of the
rainforest floor, the gaboon viper
becomes almost invisible. Many
snakes have colours and patterns
that match their surroundings.

41

Reproduction

Snakes do not live as families, and parents do not look after their young. Males and females come together to mate, and pairs may stay together for the breeding season. Most snakes are ready to mate when they are between two and five years old. In cooler climates, snakes usually mate in spring so that their young have time to feed and grow before the winter starts. In tropical climates, snakes often mate before the rainy season, when there is plenty of food for their young. Male snakes find females by following their scent trails.

flowerpot snake
(Typhlops braminus)

▶ **FIGHTING**
Male adders fight to test which one is the stronger. They rear up and face each other, then twist their necks together. Each snake tries to push the other to the ground. In the end, one of them gives up.

▲ **NO MATE**
Scientists believe that female flowerpot snakes can produce young without males. This is useful when they move to new areas, as one snake can start a new colony. However, all the young are the same, and if conditions change, the snakes cannot adapt and may die out.

spur

◀ **SNAKE SPURS**
Both boa and python males have small spurs on their bodies. These are the remains of back legs that have disappeared as snakes have developed over millions of years. A male uses its spur to scratch or tickle the female during courtship, or to fight with other males. Females' spurs are usually smaller.

▲ WRESTLING MATCH

These male Indian rat snakes are fighting to see which is the stronger. The winner stands a better chance of mating. The snakes hiss and strike out, but they seldom get hurt.

▶ SIMILARITIES AND DIFFERENCES

No one knows why the male and female of the snake shown here have such different head shapes. In fact, male and female snakes of the same species usually look similar because snakes rely on scent rather than sight to find a mate.

male

(langaha nasuta)

female

◀ MATING

When a female anaconda is ready to mate, she lets the male coil his tail around hers. The male has to place his sperm inside the female's body to fertilize her eggs. The eggs can then develop into baby snakes.

43

Eggs

Some snakes lay eggs and some give birth to fully developed, or live, young. Egg-laying snakes include cobras and pythons. A few weeks after mating, the female looks for a safe, warm, moist place to lay between 6 and 40 eggs. This may be under a rotting log, in sandy soil, under a rock or in a compost heap. Most snakes cover their eggs and leave them to hatch by themselves. A few snakes stay with their eggs to protect them from predators and the weather. However, once the eggs hatch, all snakes abandon their young.

▲ BEACH BIRTH

Sea kraits are the only sea snakes to lay eggs. They often do this in caves, above the water level.

► EGG CARE

This female python has piled up her eggs and coiled herself around them to protect them from predators. The female Indian python twitches her muscles to warm up her body. The extra heat helps the young to develop. Snake eggs need to be kept at a certain temperature to develop properly.

◄ LAYING EGGS

The Oenpellis python lays rounded eggs. The eggs of smaller snakes are usually long and thin to fit inside their smaller body. Some snakes lay long, thin eggs when they are young, but more rounded eggs when they grow larger.

Did you know? The mud snake lays over 100 eggs at a time.

▼ CHILDREN'S PYTHON MASS HATCHING

As they hatch, these children's pythons flatten their egg shells. A snake's egg shell is leathery, not brittle like the shell of a bird's egg. Birds' eggs would break into pieces if they were squashed. A snake's egg is not completely watertight, so it is laid in a moist place to keep it from drying up.

children's pythons (*Liasis childreni*)

▼ HIDDEN EGGS

Eggs are hidden from predators in the soil, or under rocks and logs. Eggs are never completely buried, as the young need to breathe air that flows through the outer shell.

▲ HOT SPOTS

This female grass snake has laid her eggs in a warm pile of rotting plants.

45

Focus on Hatching

About two to four months after the adults mate, the baby snakes hatch out of their eggs. Inside the egg, the baby snake feeds on the yolk, which is full of nutrition. Once the snake has fully developed and the yolk has been consumed, the snake is ready to hatch. All the eggs in a clutch tend to hatch at the same time. A few days later, the baby snake wriggles away to start life without its parents.

1 Eight weeks after being laid, these rat snake eggs are hatching. While they developed inside the egg, each baby rat snake fed on its yolk. A day or so before hatching, the yolk sac was drawn inside the snake's body.

2 The baby snake has become restless, twisting inside its shell. It is now fully developed and cannot get enough oxygen through its shell. A snake's egg has an almost watertight shell, but water and gases, such as oxygen, pass in and out of it through tiny holes (pores). As the baby snake prepares to hatch, it cuts a slit in the shell with a sharp egg tooth on its snout. This egg tooth will drop off a few hours after hatching.

3 After it has broken through the shell, the baby snake has a rest. It pokes its nose through the slit in the egg to breathe the air and take a first look at the strange and exciting world outside.

4 All the eggs in this clutch have hatched at the same time (a clutch is a set of eggs laid by a snake). After making the first slits in their leathery shells, the baby snakes will not crawl out right away. They poke their heads out of their eggs to taste the air with their forked tongues. If they are disturbed, they will slide back inside the shell where they feel safe. They may stay inside the shell for a few days.

Did you know? Some snakes lay as many as 100 eggs in one clutch.

5 Eventually, the baby snake slithers out of the egg. It may be as much as seven times longer than the egg because it was coiled up inside.

Pope's tree viper
(*Trimeresurus popeorum*)

▲ **TREE BIRTH**

Tree snakes often give birth in the branches. The membrane around each baby snake sticks to the leaves and helps stop the baby from falling out of the branches to the ground.

Giving Birth

Some snakes give birth to fully developed or live young. Snakes that do this include boas, rattlesnakes and adders. The eggs develop inside the mother's body surrounded by see-through bags, called membranes. While the baby snake is developing inside the mother, it gets its food from the yolk of the egg. The babies are born after a labour that may last for hours. Anything from 6 to 50 babies are born at a time. At birth, they are still inside their membranes.

▲ **BIRTH PLACE**

This female sand viper has chosen a quiet, remote spot to give birth to her young. Snakes usually give birth in a hidden place, where the young are safe from enemies.

▶ **BABY BAGS**

These red-tailed boas have just been born. They are still inside their see-through bags. The bags are made of a clear, thin, tough membrane, rather like the one inside the shell of a hen's egg.

Did you know? Newborn anacondas are only 6cm long.

► **BREAKING FREE**

This baby rainbow boa has just pushed its head through its surrounding membrane. Snakes have to break free of their baby bags on their own. Each baby has an egg tooth to cut a slit in the membrane and wriggle out. The babies usually do this a few seconds after birth.

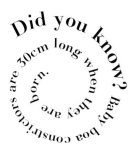

Did you know? Baby boa constrictors are 30cm long when they are born.

◄ **NEW BABY**

A red-tailed boa has broken free of its egg sac, which is in the front of the picture. The baby's colours are bright. Some newborn babies crawl off straight away, while others stay with their mother for a few days.

◄ **COLOUR CHANGE**

This vivid red baby is an emerald tree boa. As it grows up, it will turn green. Although boas and pythons are very similar snakes in some ways, one of the main differences between them is that boas give birth to live young while pythons lay eggs.

Did you know? Timber rattlesnake mothers defend their newborn babies for a few days.

emerald tree boa
(Epicrates cenchria)

Growth and Development

The size of baby snakes when they are born or when they hatch from their eggs, how much they eat and the climate around them all affect their rate of growth. In warm climates, snakes may double or triple their length in just one year. Some snakes are mature and almost fully grown after three to five years, but slow growth may continue throughout their lives. Young snakes shed their skin more often than adults because they are growing quickly. While they are growing, young snakes are easy prey for animals such as birds, racoons, toads and rats.

▼ **FAST FOOD**
Like all young snakes, this Burmese python must eat as much as possible in order to grow quickly. Young snakes eat smaller prey than their parents, such as ants, earthworms and flies.

▲ **DEADLY BABY**
This baby European adder can give a nasty bite soon after hatching. Luckily, its venom is not very strong.

mother European adder

baby European adder

▲ **MOTHER AND BABY**
European adders give birth in summer. The young must grow fast so that they are big enough to survive winter hibernation.

50

Burmese python
(Python molurus bivittatus)

Heracles the Strong
Heracles was the son of Zeus, king of the ancient Greek gods. His mother was Alcmene, an ordinary human being. Zeus's wife, Hera, was jealous of Alcmene's baby. She sent two poisonous snakes to kill Heracles as he slept. But Heracles was strong and killed the snakes by strangling them with his bare hands.

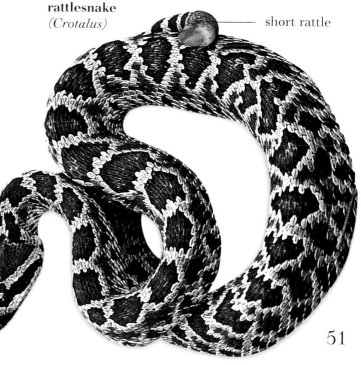

rattlesnake
(Crotalus) — short rattle

▲ DIET CHANGE

Many young Amazon tree boas live on islands in the West Indies. They start off by feeding on lizards, but as they grow they switch to feeding on birds and mammals.

▶ RATTLE AGE

You cannot tell the age of a rattlesnake by counting the sections of its rattle because several sections may be added each year and pieces of the rattle may break off.

51

Where Snakes Live

Snakes live on every continent except
Antarctica. They are most common in deserts
and rainforests. They cannot survive in very
cold places because they use the heat around
them to make their bodies work. This is why
most snakes live in warm places where the
temperature is high enough for them to stay
active day and night. In cooler places, snakes
may spend the cold winter months asleep.
This is called hibernation.

▲ **GRASSLANDS**
The European grass snake is one of
the few snakes to live on grasslands,
where there is little food or shelter.

◄ **MOUNTAINS**
The Pacific rattlesnake is
sometimes found in the mountains
of the western United States, often on
the lower slopes covered with
loose rock.
In general,
however,
mountains are
problem places for
snakes because of their
cold climates.

▲ **WINTER SLEEP**
Thousands of garter snakes emerge
after their winter sleep.

◀ TROPICAL RAINFORESTS

The greatest variety of snakes lives in tropical rainforests, including this Brazilian rainbow boa. There is plenty to eat, from insects, birds and bats to frogs.

▲ LIVING IN TREES

The eyelash viper lives in the Central American rainforest. The climate in rainforests is warm all year round, so snakes can stay active all the time. There are also plenty of places to live – in trees, on the forest floor, in soil and in rivers.

Brazilian rainbow boa
(Epicrates cenchria)

▶ BURROWERS

Yellow-headed worm snakes live under tree bark. Many worm, or thread, snakes live under ground where the soil is warm.

◀ DESERTS

This African puff adder lives in the Kalahari desert of southern Africa. Many snakes live in deserts because they can survive with little food and water.

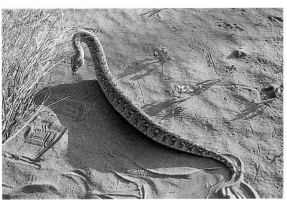

53

Tree Snakes

With their long, thin, flat bodies and pointed heads, tree snakes slide easily through the branches of tropical forests. Some can even glide from tree to tree. Tree boas and pythons have ridges on their belly scales to give them extra gripping power. Many tree snakes also have long, thin tails that coil tightly around branches. Green or brown camouflage colours keep tree snakes well hidden among the leaves and branches.

▲ COLOUR AND PATTERN

This Amazon tree boa is coloured and patterned for camouflage. Many tree snakes are green or brown with patterns that break up the outline of their body shape. Some even have patterns that look like mosses and lichens.

▲ TREE TWINS

The green tree python lives in the rainforests of New Guinea. It looks similar to the emerald tree boa and behaves in a similar way, but they are not closely related.

◄ GRASPING

In a rainforest in Costa Rica, a blunt-headed tree snake has caught a lizard. It grasps its prey firmly so that it does not fall out of the tree.

54

long-nosed whip snake
(Ahaetulla mycterizens)

Did you know? Many snakes have long tails to grip tree trunks and branches.

▲ **HEADS AND EYES**

The long-nosed whip snake opens its colourful mouth to scare away a predator. It has a long head, with a pointed snout — an ideal shape for sliding through branches.

Cook's tree boa
(Boa cookii)

▲ **VIPER REFLEXES**

The green eyelash viper has such speedy reflexes that it can catch birds as they fly through the trees. It has to hold on to its prey while its venom takes effect.

► **BODY WEIGHT**

Tree snakes have long, thin, light bodies. This helps them to stretch easily from one branch to another.

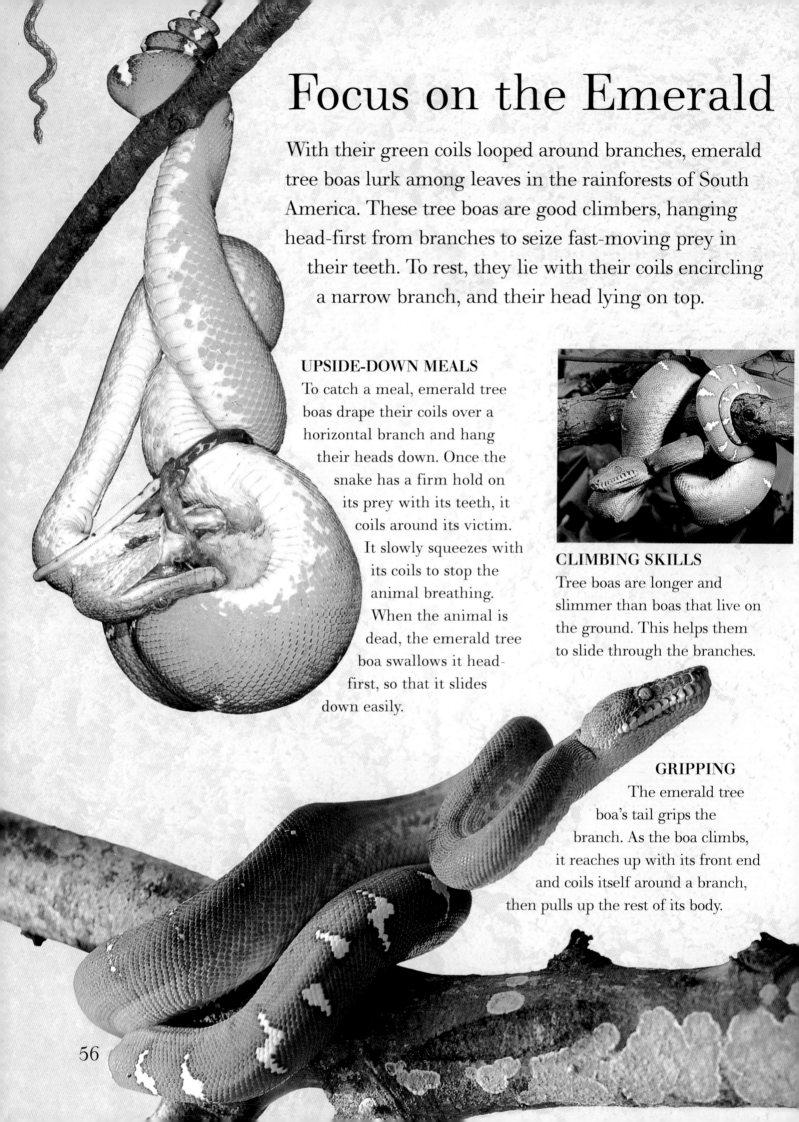

Focus on the Emerald

With their green coils looped around branches, emerald tree boas lurk among leaves in the rainforests of South America. These tree boas are good climbers, hanging head-first from branches to seize fast-moving prey in their teeth. To rest, they lie with their coils encircling a narrow branch, and their head lying on top.

UPSIDE-DOWN MEALS
To catch a meal, emerald tree boas drape their coils over a horizontal branch and hang their heads down. Once the snake has a firm hold on its prey with its teeth, it coils around its victim. It slowly squeezes with its coils to stop the animal breathing. When the animal is dead, the emerald tree boa swallows it head-first, so that it slides down easily.

CLIMBING SKILLS
Tree boas are longer and slimmer than boas that live on the ground. This helps them to slide through the branches.

GRIPPING
The emerald tree boa's tail grips the branch. As the boa climbs, it reaches up with its front end and coils itself around a branch, then pulls up the rest of its body.

Tree Boa

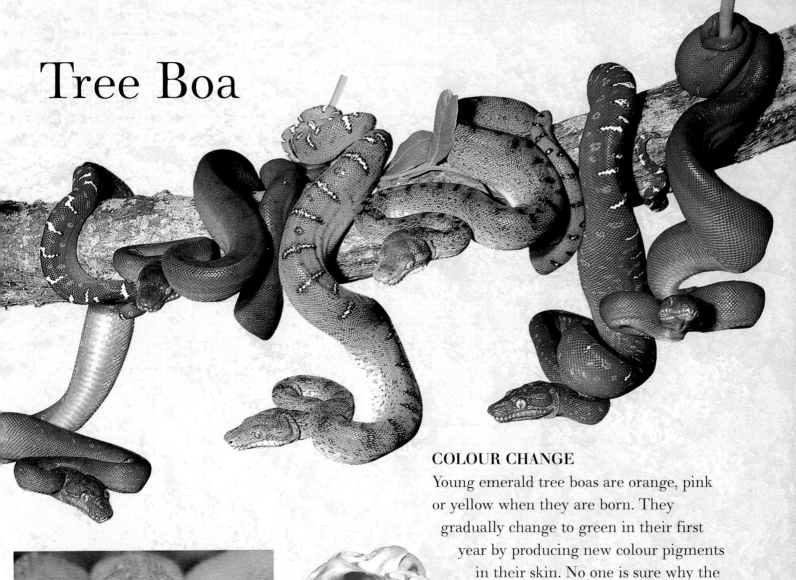

COLOUR CHANGE

Young emerald tree boas are orange, pink or yellow when they are born. They gradually change to green in their first year by producing new colour pigments in their skin. No one is sure why the young are a different colour from the adults. They may live in different places from the adults and so need a different colour for effective camouflage.

HOT LIPS

Emerald tree boas use pits on their lips to sense the heat given off by prey animals.

LETHAL JAWS

The emerald tree boa can open its mouth very wide to fit more of its prey inside. This is why the snake can feed on animals that move quickly, such as birds.

Desert Snakes

Deserts are full of snakes. This is partly because snakes can survive for a long time without food. They don't need energy from food to produce body heat because they get heat energy from their surroundings. It is also because their waterproof skins stop them losing too much water. Snakes push between rocks or down rodent burrows to escape the Sun's heat and the night's bitter cold.

◀ **SCALE SOUNDS**
If threatened, the desert horned viper makes a loud rasping sound by rubbing together jagged scales along the sides of its body. This warns predators to keep away.

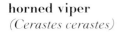

horned viper
(Cerastes cerastes)

▶ **RATTLING**
A rattlesnake shakes its rattle to warn enemies. It shakes its tail and often lifts its head off the ground. It cannot hear the buzzing noise it makes — but its enemies can.

▶ SAND SHUFFLE

The desert horned viper shuffles under the sand by rocking its body to and fro. It spreads its ribs to flatten its body and pushes its way down until it almost disappears. It strikes out at its prey from this position.

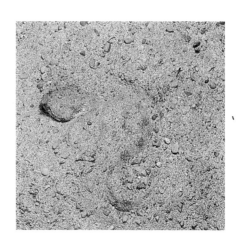

◀ SIDEWINDING

Many desert snakes, such as this Peringuey's viper, travel in a movement called sidewinding. As the snake moves, only a small part of its body touches the hot sand at any time. Sidewinding also helps to stop the snake sinking down into the loose sand.

◀ HIDDEN BOA

The colours of this sand boa make it hard for predators and prey to spot among desert rocks and sand. The sand boa's long, round body shape helps it to burrow down into the sand.

The Hopi Indians

This Native North American was a Hopi snake chief. The Hopi people used snakes in their rain dances to carry prayers to the rain gods to make rain fall on their desert lands.

Water Snakes

Some snakes live in marshy areas or at the edge of freshwater lakes and rivers. Two groups of snakes live in salty sea water. They breathe air, but they can stay underwater for a long time. Glands on their heads get rid of some of the salt from the water. Sea snakes have hollow front fangs and are very poisonous. This is because a sea snake has to subdue its prey quickly in order to avoid losing it in the depths of the sea.

◄ SENSES
A sea snake's eyes and nostrils lie toward the top of the head. This means it can take a breath without lifting its head right out of the water, and the eyes can watch out for predators about to attack.

▼ CHAMPION SWIMMER
Northern water snakes are good swimmers, rarely found far from fresh water. They feed mainly on fish, frogs, salamanders and toads. At the first sign of danger, they dive under the water.

► BREATH CONTROL
Sea snakes have a large lung, enabling them to stay underwater for a few hours at a time.

◄ HEAVY WEIGHT

The green anaconda lurks in swamps and slow-moving rivers, waiting for birds, turtles and caimans to come within reach of its strong coils. They weigh up to 227kg!

sea krait
(*Laticauda colubrina*)

▲ LAND LUBBER

The sea krait is less well adapted to the water and lays eggs on land.

61

Snake Families

Scientists have divided the 2,700 different kinds of snake into about ten groups, called families. These are the colubrids, the elapids, the vipers, the boas and pythons, the sea snakes, the sunbeam snakes, the blind snakes and worm snakes, the thread snakes, the shieldtail snakes and the false coral snakes. The snakes in each family have features in common. The biggest family is the colubrid family, with over 1,800 different species of snake.

Did you know? The viper family includes rattlesnakes, adders, asps and pit vipers.

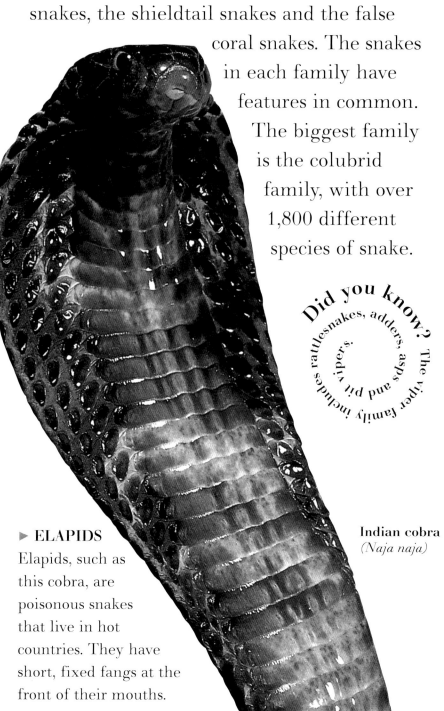

Indian cobra
(Naja naja)

▶ **ELAPIDS**
Elapids, such as this cobra, are poisonous snakes that live in hot countries. They have short, fixed fangs at the front of their mouths.

62

▲ **COLUBRIDS**
About three-quarters of all the world's snakes, including this milk snake, belong to the colubrid family. Most colubrids are not poisonous. They have no left lung or hip bones.

▲ **VIPERS**
Snakes in this family, such as the sand viper, have long, hollow fangs that can be folded back inside the mouth when they are not needed.

Classification Chart		
	Kingdom ⇩	Animalia ⇩
	Phylum ⇩	Chordata ⇩
	Class ⇩	Reptilia ⇩
	Order ⇩	Squamata ⇩
	Suborder ⇩	Ophidia ⇩
	Family ⇩	Boidae ⇩
	Genus ⇩	Boa ⇩
	Species	Boa constrictor

This chart shows how a boa constrictor is classified within the animal kingdom.

Colombian rainbow boa
(Epicrates cenchria maurus)

▶ **BOAS AND PYTHONS**
This family includes snakes that kill by constriction rather than poisoning. They have curved teeth, hip bones and tiny back leg bones.

▶ **SEA SNAKES**
Some sea snakes are born in the sea and spend all their lives there, and others spend part of their time on land. Sea snakes have flattened tails for swimming and nostrils that can be closed off underwater. Most live in warm waters, from the Red Sea to New Zealand and Japan.

◀ **SUNBEAM SNAKES**
The two members of the sunbeam family are burrowing snakes that live in Southeast Asia and southern China. Unlike most other snakes, they have two working lungs.

63

Snake Relatives

sand lizard

▲ **LIZARDS**
This sand lizard is threatening an enemy by making itself look big and scary. Lizards have movable eyelids and good eyesight. Most lizards have pointed tongues.

Snakes are part of a large group of animals called reptiles. There are about 6,000 different kinds of reptiles, nearly half of which are snakes. Other reptiles include turtles and tortoises, lizards, crocodiles and alligators. Reptiles have bony skeletons with a backbone and bodies covered in scales. They lay eggs with waterproof shells or give birth to live young. Young reptiles look like copies of their parents. Reptiles are cold-blooded and rely on their surroundings for heat, so they live mostly in warm places.

Did you know? The largest reptile in the world is the saltwater crocodile, which grows over 7 m long.

baby crocodile

◄ **CARING CROCODILES**
Crocodiles are dangerous reptiles. Yet female crocodiles make doting mothers. They guard their eggs and protect their young until they can fend for themselves.

◄ LEGLESS LIZARDS

Some burrowing lizards have tiny legs – or none at all. Snakes possibly developed from burrowing lizards, which did not need legs for sliding through soil.

Did you know? The only two poisonous lizards are the gils monster and the Mexican bearded lizard.

▼ LIZARD TAILS

Lizards, like this water dragon, generally have long tails and shed their skin in several pieces.

water dragon

▼ TORTOISES

A tortoise has a shell as well as a skeleton. The shell is made from bony plates fused to the ribs, with an outer covering of horny plates. It is useful for protection, but it is also very heavy.

tortoise

▼ BURROWING LIZARD

Worm lizards dig burrows underground with their strong, hard heads. Their nostrils close during burrowing so they do not get clogged up with soil.

worm lizard

65

Conservation

Some snakes are killed because people are afraid of them. Farmers often kill snakes to protect their farm animals and workers, although many snakes actually help farmers by eating pests. In some countries snakes are killed for food or used to make medicines. To help snakes survive, people need to take action to preserve their habitats, so that snakes can live in safety.

▲ **TROPHY**
There are still those who shoot snakes for recreation. The hunters put the snake's rattle or head on display as a trophy demonstrating their sporting achievements.

▲ **FINDING OUT MORE**
Scientists use an antenna to pick up signals from a transmitter fitted to a rattlesnake. This allows them to track the snake. The more we can learn about snakes, the easier it is to protect them.

▶ **SNAKES IN DANGER**
Snakes, such as this Dumeril's boa, are in danger of dying out. Threats include people taking them from the wild and road building in places where they live.

66

▼ ROUND-UP

This show in North America demonstrates the skill needed to capture a rattlesnake. Today, rattlesnake hunts are not as common as they once were.

▲ USING SNAKE SKINS

Snake skins have been used for many years to make jewelry. Some species have declined as a result of intensive killing for skins in some areas. Recently, countries such as Sri Lanka and India have banned the export of snake skins.

Did you know? Legend says St Patrick banished snakes from Ireland to rid the country of evil.

▼ PET SNAKES

Some people like to keep pet snakes. However, they can do very little and are not happy in captivity. Snakes can lose the ability to hunt and dislike being kept in a confined space.

BIRDS OF PREY

Most birds eat fruits and seeds but birds of prey eat meat—dead or alive. They are equipped with hooked talons, curved beaks and keen eyesight and hearing. Some birds of prey calmly wait for their victims to fly past their perch, while others hover in the air, ready to swoop down with extraordinary precision on their next meal.

Author: Robin Kerrod
Consultant: Jemima Parry Jones, M.B.E.
The National Birds of Prey Centre

What is a Bird of Prey?

There are nearly 9,000 different species of birds in the world. Most of them eat plant shoots, seeds, nuts and fruit, or small creatures such as insects and worms. However, around 400 species, called birds of prey, hunt prey with their feet or scavenge carrion (the flesh of dead animals). Birds of prey are called raptors, from the Latin *rapere* meaning "to seize", because they grip and kill their prey with sharp talons and hooked beaks. The majority of raptors hunt by day. They are called diurnal birds of prey. Day hunters include eagles, falcons and hawks, and vultures (which are scavengers). Other raptors, such as owls, are nocturnal, which means they are active at night.

▼ **HANGING AROUND**

The outstretched wings of the kestrel (*Falco tinnunculus*) face into the wind as the bird hovers above a patch of ground in search of prey. The bird also spreads its broad tail to supplement the air-catching effect of its wings.

Large, forward-facing eyes

Hooked, powerful, bill

▼ **IN A LEAGUE OF THEIR OWN**

Five young tawny owls cluster together on a branch. Owls are not closely related to the other birds of prey. They usually hunt by night instead of during the day. However, they do share certain features with the other birds of prey. They have excellent eyesight for spotting prey, sharp, hooked beaks (bills) for ripping flesh, and strong legs, with pointed, curled claws (talons) for gripping their prey.

Tawny owls
(*Strix aluco*)

HAWKEYE

The sparrowhawk has large eyes that face forwards. The bill is hooked, for tearing flesh. These are typical features of daytime hunters.

Eurasian sparrowhawk
(*Accipiter nisus*)

Wings lift in the flow of air and support the bird's weight. The primary feathers on the wing fan out.

Long, sharp, curved talons

Tail guides the bird through the air and also acts as a brake

BUILT FOR SPEED

The peregrine falcon is the one of the swiftest birds in the world, able to dive at up to 224 km/h. Its swept-back wings help it cut through the air at speed. Their shape has been copied by aircraft designers for the wings of fighter planes.

THE EAGLE HAS LANDED

In the snow-covered highlands of Scotland, a golden eagle stands over a rabbit it has just killed. Eagles kill with their talons. They are so long, sharp and deeply curved that one swipe is usually enough to kill the rabbit.

Golden eagle
(*Aquila chrysaetos*)

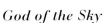

God of the Sky
Horus was one of the most important gods in ancient Egypt. He was the god of the sky and the heavens. His sacred bird was the falcon, and Horus is often represented with a human body and a falcon's head. The Egyptian hieroglyph (picture symbol) for "god" in ancient Egyptian is a falcon.

Shapes and Sizes

There are huge differences in size among birds of prey. As many as 40 pygmy falcons could perch on the outstretched wings of one Andean condor. Pygmy falcons are the smallest birds of prey, measuring as little as 20 centimetres from head to tail. The Andean condor is the biggest bird of prey, with a wingspan of some 3 metres. In most species, the female is larger than the male. In fact, in some hawk and falcon species the females are up to 50 per cent bigger than the males. This is called reverse sexual dimorphism. Most raptors look quite similar when they perch. When they fly, however, there is a great variation in wing size and shape. This usually reflects the different techniques they adopt when hunting prey and the nature of their habitat. For example, the huge wings of the Andean condor allow it to soar high above the Andes mountains.

▲ AMERICAN SCAVENGER
The turkey vulture (or turkey buzzard) is a small vulture that lives in North and South America. It grows up to 80 cm from head to tail.

Little owl
(*Athene noctua*)

▲ WELL-ROUNDED
The little owl, like other owls, has a round head and broad, rounded wings. Its body, too, has a well-rounded shape, because of its fairly loose covering of feathers. It appears to have no neck at all. The little owl is about 23 cm from head to tail.

► DIFFERENT SIZES
The female sparrowhawk can grow up to about 38 cm from head to tail. The male bird (shown here) is much smaller, reaching only about 28 cm from head to tail.

Eurasian sparrowhawk
(*Accipiter nisus*)

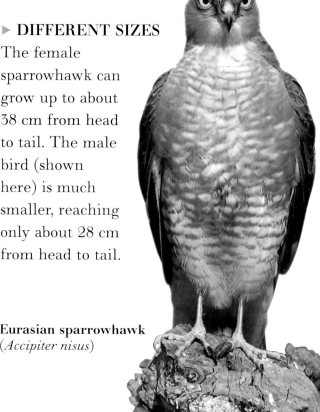

72

▶ THE BIGGEST

The magnificent Andean condor is the biggest of all birds of prey. The males grow up to 1.3 m from head to tail and can weigh more than 12 kg. The condor is a scavenger, which means that it feeds on dead animals rather than hunting live prey.

Andean condor (*Vultur gryphus*)

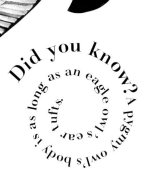

Did you know? A pygmy owl's body is as long as an eagle owl's ear tufts.

▲ COMMON BUTEOS

This common buzzard (*Buteo buteo*) is typical of the family of birds of prey known as buteos. Buteos are about 50 cm from head to tail and have long, broad wings up to 1.3 m from wing tip to wing tip. This bird is commonly found gliding high above the grasslands and woodlands of Europe and Asia in search of small mammals and reptiles.

▲ FISH-EATING EAGLE

The bald eagle (*Haliaeetus leucocephalus*) is instantly recognizable by its snowy white head and tail. It is an impressive bird, growing up to 1 m from head to tail. The bird's long talons enable it to pluck fish from the surface of rivers and lakes in North America.

▶ STANDING TALL

The tallest and most unusual bird of prey is the secretary bird of Africa. It stands up to 1.2 m tall, and its wings can span more than 2 m. It can soar in the sky like other birds of prey, but most of the time it walks on the ground on its long legs.

Secretary bird (*Sagittarius serpentarius*)

73

How the Body Works

Birds of prey are supreme fliers. Like other birds, they have powerful chest and wing muscles to move their wings. Virtually the whole body is covered with feathers to make it smooth and streamlined and able to slip easily through the air. The bones are very light, and some have a honeycomb structure, which makes them lighter still. Birds of prey differ from other birds in a number of ways, particularly in their powerful bills (beaks) and feet, which are well adapted for their life as hunters. Also unlike most other birds, they regurgitate (cough up) pellets. These contain the parts of their prey they cannot digest.

NAKED NECK
A Ruppell's vulture feeds on a zebra carcass in the Masai Mara region of eastern Africa. Like many vultures, it has a naked neck, which it can thrust deep inside the carcass. As a result, it can feed without getting its feathers too covered in blood.

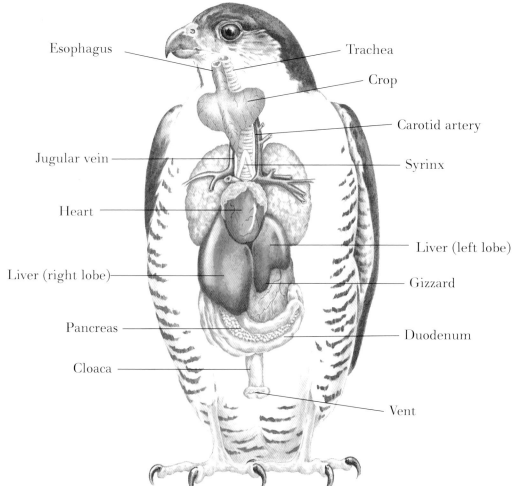

Esophagus
Trachea
Crop
Carotid artery
Jugular vein
Syrinx
Heart
Liver (left lobe)
Liver (right lobe)
Gizzard
Pancreas
Duodenum
Cloaca
Vent

BODY PARTS
Underneath their feathery covering, birds of prey have a complex system of internal organs. Unlike humans, most birds have a crop to store food in before digestion. They also have a gizzard to grind up hard particles of food, such as bone, and to start the process of making a pellet. Birds also have a syrinx (the bird equivalent of the human vocal cord).

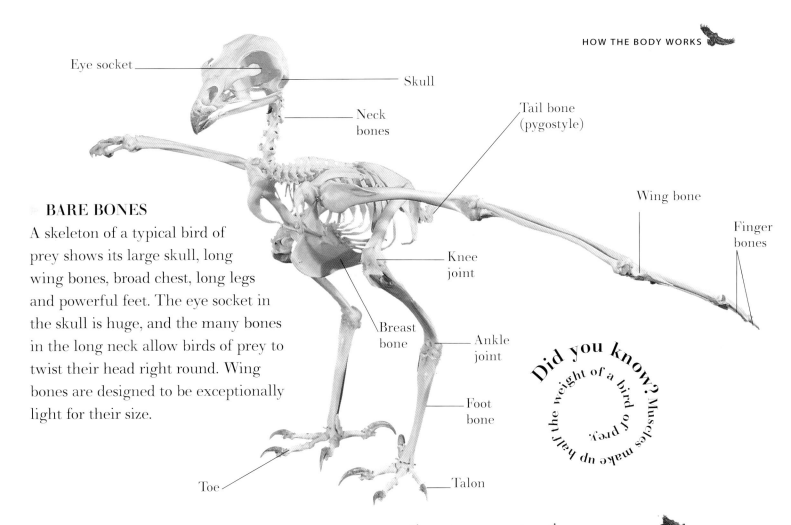

Eye socket

Skull

Neck bones

Tail bone (pygostyle)

Wing bone

Finger bones

Knee joint

Breast bone

Ankle joint

Foot bone

Toe

Talon

Did you know? Muscles make up half the weight of a bird of prey.

BARE BONES

A skeleton of a typical bird of prey shows its large skull, long wing bones, broad chest, long legs and powerful feet. The eye socket in the skull is huge, and the many bones in the long neck allow birds of prey to twist their head right round. Wing bones are designed to be exceptionally light for their size.

BACK TO FRONT

This peregrine falcon appears to have eyes in the back of its head! Its body is facing away, but its eyes are looking straight into the camera. All birds of prey can twist their heads right round like this, because they have many more vertebrae than mammals. They can see in any direction without moving the body, but they cannot move their eyeballs in their sockets.

Peregrine falcon
(*Falco peregrinus*)

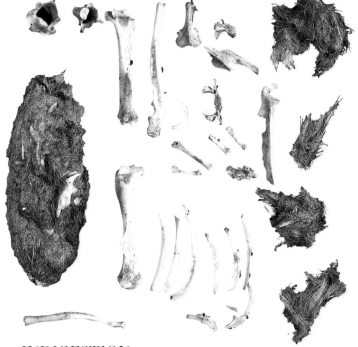

INDIGESTION

On the left of the picture above is the regurgitated (coughed-up) pellet of a barn owl, and on the right are the indigestible parts it contained. The pellet is about 5 cm long. From its contents we can tell that the owl has just eaten a small mammal, because the pellet contains scraps of fur and fragments of bone.

75

The Senses

Humans rely on five senses to find out about the world. They are sight, hearing, smell, taste and touch. However, most birds live using just the two senses of sight and hearing. In birds of prey, sight is by far the most important sense for finding and hunting the prey they need to survive. Their eyes are exceptionally large in relation to the size of their head, and they are set in the skull so that they look forwards. This binocular (two-eyed) forward vision enables them to judge distances accurately when hunting. Owls have particularly large eyes that are well adapted for seeing in dim light. They are equally dependent on hearing to find prey in the dark. Some harriers and hawks use their keen sense of hearing to hunt, too. Birds' ear openings are quite small. They are set back from the eyes and cannot be seen because they are covered in feathers.

Common buzzard (*Buteo buteo*)

◢ OPEN WIDE

A common buzzard opens its mouth wide to make its distinctive mewing call. This bird has extremely large eyes in relation to its body, so it has excellent eyesight. The forward-facing eyes give it good stereoscopic (3D) vision and the ability to pinpoint the exact position of a mouse in the grass 100 m away.

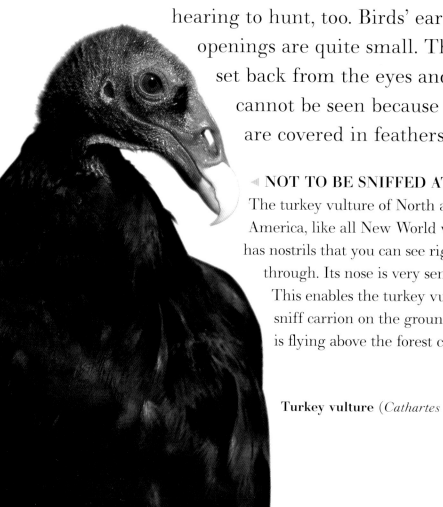

◂ NOT TO BE SNIFFED AT

The turkey vulture of North and South America, like all New World vultures, has nostrils that you can see right through. Its nose is very sensitive. This enables the turkey vulture to sniff carrion on the ground while it is flying above the forest canopy.

Turkey vulture (*Cathartes aura*)

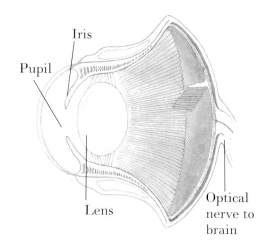

Iris

Pupil

Lens

Optical nerve to brain

◢ OWL EYE

The owl has exceptional eyesight. Its eye is very long, unlike the spherical human eye. The tubular shape of the owl's eye allows it to spot its prey from far away.

Spotted eagle owl (*Bubo africanus*)

FORWARD FACE

The African spotted eagle owl has big eyes. The pupil (centre) and lens are especially large to allow more light to enter and provide the owl with good night vision. The eyes are set in a flat facial disc. The earlike projections on top of the owl's head are actually ornamental tufts of feathers used for display. The true ears are hidden under stiff feathers at either side of the facial disc. They are sensitive to the slightest noise, which helps the owl locate its prey in the dark.

ON THE LOOKOUT

This large falcon, called a lanner, is soaring high in the sky on outstretched wings, looking down with its sharp eyes on the scene below. If the lanner sees a flying bird, it will fold back its wings and dive on the unsuspecting bird. The lanner will hit the bird at high speed and usually break its neck. Then it will either snatch the bird in mid-air or pick it up off the ground.

MONTAGU'S EYEBROW

Montagu's harrier is a slender, long-legged hawk with an owl-like facial ruff. The eyes are surrounded by a small bony ridge covered in feathers, called a supraorbital ridge. It probably helps protect the harrier's eyes from attack when the bird goes hunting, and may also act as a shield against the sun's rays when it is flying.

Montagu's harrier (*Circus pygargus*)

77

Wings and Flight

The wings of most birds work in the same way. Strong pectoral (chest) muscles make the wings flap and drive the bird through the air. As it moves, the wings lift in the flow of air and support the bird's weight. The bird is now flying. All birds have differently shaped wings that are adapted to their way of life. Large birds of prey, such as vultures, spend much of their time soaring high in the sky. These birds have long, broad wings that glide on air currents. The smaller hawks, such as the sparrowhawk, have short, rounded wings and a long tail for rapid, zigzagging flight through woodland habitats. A bird's tail is also important for flying. It acts much like a ship's rudder, steadying the bird's body and guiding it through the air. It can be fanned out to give extra lift and also helps the bird to slow down when landing.

WING FINGERS
An African fish eagle takes to the air. Like other eagles, it has broad wings and fingered wing tips, seen plainly here. The "fingers" reduce air turbulence around the wings, giving better lift.

Mauritius kestrel
(*Falco punctatus*)

AGILE BIRD
The Mauritius kestrel has a broad tail and, for a falcon, fairly short wings. These two features help it to maneuver well in the woodland habitat in which it lives. It lives on the island of Mauritius, in the Indian Ocean.

DROPPING IN
A sparrowhawk (*Accipter nisus*) is poised to seize a bird it has just spotted. It has short, rounded wings and a long tail. The sparrowhawk's wings beat rapidly and provide enough speed to surprise its unsuspecting prey.

Eagle of the Gods

In Greek mythology, the eagle was the favored bird of the mighty Zeus. Zeus was god of the sky, lord of the winds and rains, and king of the gods. He is often depicted holding a thunderbolt in his right hand, with an eagle standing at his feet. Here we see him riding in a chariot, drawn by a pair of his sacred birds.

LIKE AN ARROW

The sharply pointed wings tell us that this bird is a falcon. In fact, it is a lanner falcon. A bird can fly extremely fast with pointed wings because the wings cut through the air and offer less wind resistance. Lanner falcons hunt in open ground and use pure speed to catch slower-flying birds.

Lanner falcon
(*Falco biarmicus*)

BUILT TO SOAR

A white-backed vulture soars high in the sky with its broad wings fully outstretched on the lookout for carcasses on the ground. In the right climate, the vulture can remain in the air for a long time, because its wings provide plenty of lift.

READY, SET, GO

A young male kestrel takes off in a multiple-exposure photograph. First the bird thrusts its body forward and raises its wings. Its wings extend and beat downward, pushing slightly backward. As the air is forced back, the bird is driven forward. At the same time, air moving past the wings gives the bird the lift it needs to keep itself airborne.

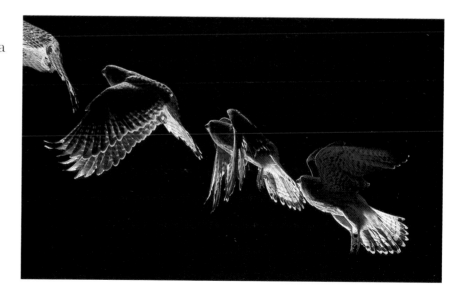

Focus on

1 A Harris' hawk (*Parabuteo unicinctus*) perches on a branch on the lookout for prey such as reptiles and small mammals. This native of South and Central America and the southern United States is also called the bay-winged hawk because of the rust-brown (bay) bars on its shoulders. It has the relatively short, rounded wings and long tail typical of most small hawks.

Most of the smaller species of hawk have developed wings that enable them to fly at fast speeds over short distances. Larger hawks have broader, longer wings. These allow the birds to soar and glide in the air whilst scanning the ground below for their prey. Every species favours a different flying technique. For example, sparrowhawks twist and turn with ease as they manoeuvre among the many trees in the woodlands in which they are found. High-speed photography allows us to follow the action as the Harris' hawk shown here takes to the air.

2 Now the hawk is getting ready to fly. It leans forwards and begins to raise its wings. It tenses its leg muscles, ready to thrust itself from the perch. The bird's distinctive red thighs and white rump, and the white patches on the underwing, are clearly visible.

3 The hawk lifts its wings, and the primaries (the flight feathers at the end of the wings) fan out. It pushes its legs against the perch to take off.

Hawk Flight

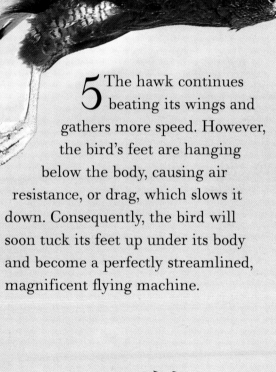

4 With a powerful downbeat of its wings and a final push with its legs, the hawk thrusts its body from the perch and begins to travel forwards through the air. As the air flows past the wings, it makes them lift and so supports the bird's body. The tail fans out and downwards to provide extra lift. The bird is now airborne.

5 The hawk continues beating its wings and gathers more speed. However, the bird's feet are hanging below the body, causing air resistance, or drag, which slows it down. Consequently, the bird will soon tuck its feet up under its body and become a perfectly streamlined, magnificent flying machine.

Did you know? Sacs in a bird's body fill with air to help it stay airborne.

Bill and Talons

The bill and talons of birds of prey are well adapted for killing and feeding on prey or scavenging on the remains of carcasses. Typically the bill is hooked and sharp. However, it is not generally used for killing, but for tearing flesh. Raptors also use their bills to pluck the feathers from birds they catch. Most birds of prey use their feet for the kill. Their toes are tipped with long, sharp, curved talons. When a bird swoops on its prey, the toes clamp round the prey's body and the talons sink into the flesh. The prey is quickly crushed to death. Small birds of prey, such as many falcon species, have less powerful leg muscles and may not always kill their prey this way. So the bird may have to finish it off with a bite. For this purpose, they have a notch (called a tomial tooth) in the upper part of the bill.

Indian honey buzzard (*Pernis ptilorhyncus*)

▲ INSECT-EATER
The bill of the Indian honey buzzard is relatively small and delicate compared with that of most other birds of prey. The honey buzzard has no need for a strong bill because it feeds mainly on insects and the larvae of wasps and bees.

▶ EGG HEAD
The Egyptian vulture's hooked bill is too weak to break into a large carcass without the aid of larger vultures. However, its long bill is ideal for breaking eggs, one of its favourite foods. In contrast to this bird's fine head plummage, other vultures have bare heads and necks. This prevents them from covering their feathers with blood when they reach deep inside a carcass to feed.

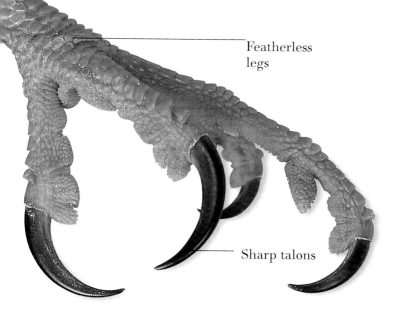

Featherless
legs

Sharp talons

▲ SPINDLY LEGS

The legs of the sparrowhawk are long and
slender and lack feathers. Both the toes and
talons are long. As it homes in on a small bird,
the sparrowhawk thrusts its legs forwards, with
both feet spread wide. It then snaps its toes and
talons around the prey's body, and captures it in
a deadly grip. The sparrowhawk then flies off
to land and feed on its catch.

▲ FEATHER TROUSERS

Like most owls, the great horned owl of North
America has soft feathers covering its legs and feet,
as well as its body. They help keep its flight silent.

▲ FEET FIRST

The strong feet of the American bald eagle
are geared to catching fish, the main part of
the bird's diet. Its talons are sharp and
curved. The American bald eagle's feet are
powerful enough to cope with a struggling
pacific salmon, sometimes weighing as much
as the bird itself.

Horrific Harpies
The harpy
eagle is one
of the most
formidable
birds of prey.
It takes its
name from
the Harpies
of Greek
mythology. These were
winged monsters that brought
violent winds. They had
women's heads, pale
with hunger, and the
bodies and sharp talons of
eagles. They attacked people and
stole or fouled their food.

Hunting on the Wing

Sparrowhawk
(*Accipiter nisus*)

Birds of prey hunt in different ways. Many smaller raptors and owls sit on a perch and simply wait for a meal to appear on the ground or fly past. This is called still hunting. Other birds search for prey by flying low over the open ground, or in and out of cover, such as a clump of trees. Kestrels are among the birds that hover in the air while looking for prey, and then swoop down suddenly on it. On the other hand, peregrines are noted for their spectacular dives, or stoops. With wings almost folded, they dive on their prey from a great height, accelerating up to hundreds of kilometres an hour. Their aim is to strike the prey at high speed to kill it instantly. The peregrine either snatches its prey from the air, or picks it up off the ground.

▲ **SURPRISE, SURPRISE**
The sparrowhawk uses surprise and speed to make a kill. It flies under cover until it spots a potential meal, then dashes out into the open to snatch up its unsuspecting prey at speed.

◄ **PLUCKY EAGLE**
An American bald eagle plucks a cattle egret it has just killed, making a change from its usual diet of fish. Most birds of prey pluck the feathers from birds they have caught before eating, as they cannot digest them. Owls are the only birds to swallow their prey whole.

Bald eagle
(*Haliaeetus leucocephalus*)

84

Buzzard
(*Buteo buteo*)

◀ **RABBIT RELISH**
A common buzzard stands guard over the rabbit it has just killed. Over grassland, the buzzard hunts on the wing, sometimes hovering like a kestrel. Where there are trees or rocks, it may perch on a high point for hours until it sights prey. The buzzard then swoops down quickly upon it.

▲ **IN HOT PURSUIT**
An African harrier hawk chases doves along the riverbank. Such chases more often than not end in failure. This hawk is about the same size as a typical harrier, but it has longer wings.

▼ **IT'S A COVER-UP**
Spreading out its wings, a kestrel tries to cover up the mouse it is preparing to eat on its feeding post. This behaviour is known as mantling, and is common among birds of prey. They do it to hide their food from other hungry birds, in case they try to rob them.

▼ **MAKING A MEAL OF IT**
A kestrel tucks into its kill on its favourite feeding post. The bird holds the prey with its feet and claws and tears the flesh into small pieces with its sharp bill. It swallows small bones, but often discards big ones. Later it regurgitates (brings up) pellets containing the bits of its prey it was unable to digest.

Kestrel
(*Falco tinnunculus*)

The Hunted

Birds of prey hunt all kinds of animals. Many prey on other birds, including sparrows, starlings and pigeons, which are usually taken in the air. Certain birds prey on small mammals, such as rabbits, lemmings, rats, mice and voles, and some of the larger eagles will even take larger mammals. The Philippine eagle and the harpy eagles of South America pluck monkeys from the rainforest canopy. These eagles are massive birds, with bodies a metre long. Serpent eagles and secretary birds feast on snakes and other reptiles. Small birds of prey often feed on insects and worms. Most species will also supplement their diet by scavenging on carrion (the meat of dead animals) whenever they find it.

▲ **INSECT INSIDE**

A lesser kestrel prepares to eat a grasshopper it has just caught on a rooftop in Spain. This kestrel lives mainly on insects. It catches grasshoppers and beetles on the ground, and all kinds of flying insects whilst in flight. When there are plenty of insects, flocks of lesser kestrels feed together. Unlike the larger common kestrel, the lesser kestrel does not hover when hunting.

Golden eagle
(*Aquila chrysaetos*)

◄ **GOLDEN HUNTER**

A golden eagle stands guard over the squirrel it has just caught. The golden eagle usually hunts low down. It flushes out prey – mainly rabbits, hares and grouse, which it catches and kills on the ground. Whenever they get the chance, golden eagles will also eat carrion.

Martial eagle
(*Polemaetus bellicosus*)

▲ REPTILIAN SNACK

A martial eagle stands over its lizard kill in the Kruger National Park, South Africa. This is Africa's biggest eagle, capable of taking prey as big as a kuda (a small antelope).

▼ SNAIL SPECIALIST

A snail kite eyes its next meal. This is the most specialist feeder among birds of prey, eating only freshwater snails. It breeds in the Everglades National Park, Florida, USA.

Did you know? 12 species of birds of prey eat only insects.

The Fabulous Roc

In the famous tales of The Arabian Nights, Sinbad the Sailor encountered enormous birds called rocs. They looked like eagles, but were gigantic in size, and preyed on elephants and other large beasts. In this picture, the fearsome rocs are dropping huge boulders on Sinbad's ship in an attempt to finally destroy him.

▲ COBRA KILLER

A pale chanting goshawk has caught and killed a yellow cobra. The chanting goshawks earned their name because of their noisy calls in the breeding season. The African plains are the hunting grounds of both the pale and the dark chanting goshawks, which feed mainly on reptiles, such as lizards and snakes.

Snail kite
(*Rostrhamus sociabilis*)

87

Feuding and Fighting

Birds often squabble over food. Some birds of prey harry (intimidate) other raptors that have already made a kill and try to force them to drop it. This behaviour is called piracy. Sometimes birds of prey are attacked by the birds that they often prey on. A number of small birds may join forces against a larger adversary and give chase, usually calling loudly. This is known as mobbing and it generally serves to confuse and irritate the raptor and also warns off other prey in the area.

Birds of prey must also defend their nests against predators. The eggs and chicks of harriers and other ground-nesting raptors are especially vulnerable to attack. Nesting adults will often fly at intruders and try to chase them off.

▲ **SCRAP IN THE SNOW**

On the snowy shores of the Kamchatka Peninsula, in northeast Russia, these sea eagles are fighting over a fish. A Steller's sea eagle, the biggest of all sea eagles, is shown on the right, with its huge wings outstretched. Its opponents, struggling in the snow, are white-tailed eagles. The two kinds of sea eagles are bound to meet and fight, because they occupy a similar habitat and feed on similar prey – fish, birds and small mammals.

◀ **FISH FIGHT**

Two common buzzards fight over a fish they have both spotted. Buzzards do not go fishing like ospreys, but they will feed on dead fish washed up on river banks. Buzzards, like many other raptors, will eat carrion as well as their preferred food of small mammals, such as rabbits, and the worms and beetles they find on the ground.

Common buzzards
(*Buteo buteo*)

▶ UNDER THREAT

On the plains of Africa, a dead animal carcass attracts not only vultures, but other scavengers as well. Here, a jackal is trying to get a look-in, but a lappet-faced vulture is warning it off with outstretched wings.

Did you know? Hunters once used eagle owls as bait to attract mobbing birds into range.

Jay
(*Garrulus glandarius*)

▲ CLEVER MIMIC

When a jay spots a predator, such as a bird of prey, it gives out an alarm call or mimics the predator's own call to warn off other jays.

▲ IN HOT PURSUIT

An osprey has seen this pelican dive into the water and assumes that it now has a fish in its pouch. So it gives chase. Time and again, the osprey will fly straight at the pelican and scare it so much that it will finally release the fish from its pouch.

▼ SAFETY IN NUMBERS

A number of crows have ganged up to mob a steppe eagle. They are bold enough to perch dangerously close to their enemy, calling loudly to persuade it to move on. Although the eagle would be more than a match for its tormentors, it might fly off just to escape aggravation.

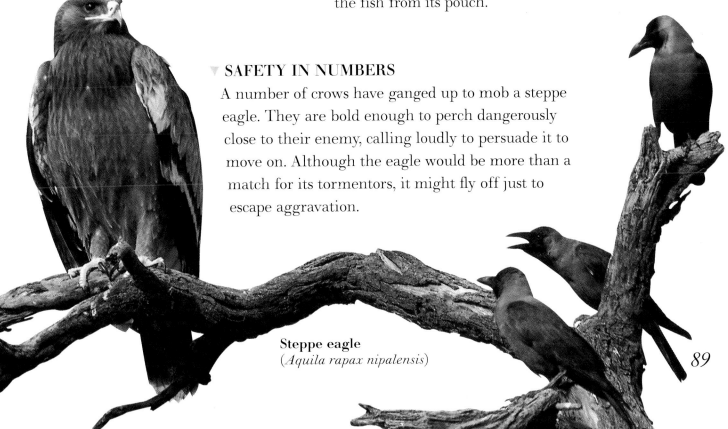

Steppe eagle
(*Aquila rapax nipalensis*)

The Night Hunters

Owls are the supreme night hunters, their bodies well adapted for hunting in the dark. For one thing, they fly silently. The flight feathers on their wings are covered with a fine down to muffle the sound of air passing through them. The owl's eyes are particularly adapted for night vision. They contain many more rods than the eyes of other species. Rods are the structures that make eyes sensitive to light. The owl's hearing is superb, too. The rings of fine feathers owls have around each eye help channel sounds into the ears. The ears themselves are surrounded by flaps of skin that can be moved to pinpoint exactly the sources of sounds. A few other raptors also hunt after sundown. They include the bat hawk of Africa and Asia, which eats bats, swallows and insects whilst in flight.

▲ GET A GRIP
Like all owls, the barn owl has powerful claws for attacking and gripping prey. The outer toe can be moved backwards and forwards to change grip.

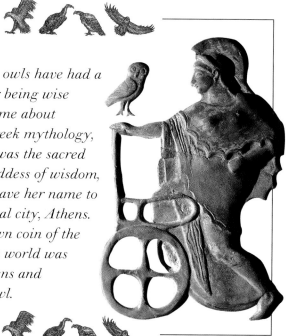

Wise Owl
For centuries, owls have had a reputation for being wise birds. This came about because in Greek mythology, the little owl was the sacred bird of the goddess of wisdom, Athena. She gave her name to Greece's capital city, Athens. The best-known coin of the ancient Greek world was issued in Athens and featured an owl.

▲ ROUNDHEAD
Of all the owls, the barn owl has the most prominent round face – properly called a facial disc. This gives it a rather ghostly appearance. The disc is formed of short, stiff feathers.

▲ BIG OWL

A European eagle owl stands over a red fox left for it as bait. It looks round warily before beginning to eat. The eagle owl is a fierce predator, and will hunt prey as big as a young roe deer. It is a large bird, growing up to 70 cm long, powerfully built, and with long ear tufts.

▼ MOUTHFUL

A barn owl carries off a mouse it has just caught. Owls carry prey in their bills, unlike the other birds of prey, which carry it in their claws. Barn owls are found throughout most of the world and in many kinds of habitat – moorland, desert, forest and farmland.

Barn owl
(*Tyto alba*)

▶ WHAT A HOOTER

A mouse is carried off by a tawny owl. The long hooting call of the tawny owl can be heard in woodlands, parks and gardens across Europe.

▲ PEEKABOO

A burrowing owl peers out of its nest hole. These small, long-legged birds live in the prairies and grasslands of the New World, from Canada to the tip of South America. They often take over the abandoned holes of other burrowers, such as prairie dogs.

Focus on

1 This owl is waiting for a rustle in the undergrowth. Suddenly it hears something. It swivels its head, and its sensitive ears pinpoint exactly where the sound is coming from. Then it sees a mouse, rummaging among the leaf litter on the ground for grubs and insects.

2 Keeping its eyes glued on its potential meal, the owl launches itself into the air. It brings its body forwards, pushes off the post with its feet and opens its wings. Just a few metres away, the mouse carries on rummaging for food. It has heard nothing and is busy searching out a tasty insect in the leaf litter on the ground.

The barn owl is found on all continents except Antarctica. It is easily recognizable because of its white, heart-shaped facial disc. Its eyes are relatively small for an owl, but it can still see well at night. It hunts as much by ear as by eye. Its hearing is particularly keen, because the feathers on its exceptionally well-developed facial disc channel sounds into its ears with great precision. The owl featured here is "still-hunting", watching for prey from a favourite perch. However, barn owls often hunt while flying. They cruise slowly and silently back and forth over their feeding grounds until they hear or spy prey, then swoop down silently for the kill.

the Silent Swoop

3 The owl makes a beeline for its prey with powerful beats of its wings. Even though it is travelling quite fast, it still makes no sound. The owl has dense, soft feathers covering its wings and legs. These feathers silence the flow of air as it passes through them. This helps the owl to muffle its flight and to concentrate on the sounds that the mouse makes as the bird draws closer to its prey.

5 Now only a few centimetres above the ground, the owl thrusts its feet forwards, claws spread wide, and drops on to its prey. At the same time, it spreads out its wings and tail to slow down its approach. The hunter's aim is deadly. Its talons close round the mouse and crush it to death. Then the owl picks up the dead mouse in its beak and returns to its perch. The owl will swallow the mouse head-first.

4 The mouse at last begins to sense that something is wrong as the owl approaches. For an instant it is glued to the spot in fear. Then it starts to run for its life. However, the owl is more than a match for it. With its rounded wings and broad tail, it is able to twist and turn in the air with ease, following every change of direction of the scuttling mouse.

93

Fishing Birds

Many birds of prey will eat dead fish when they find it on the river bank and shore. However, some specialize in plucking live fish from the water. Outstanding among the fishing birds is the osprey, found around rivers and lakes throughout the world, except in the polar regions. In many areas, the osprey competes for its food with various species of sea or fish eagles, such as the magnificent bald eagle of North America. All these fishing raptors are large. They have strong, arched bills, long talons, and rough scales on their feet, which help them grip their slippery prey. Their pale underparts imitate the bright sky and camouflage them from the fish below.

▲ BALD FISHER
An American bald eagle rests on a branch with a fish it has killed. It is the only fishing eagle in the Americas. The white feathers on its head and neck make the bird look bald from a distance.

▲ FISH OWL
Some owls go fishing, too. This Pel's fishing owl, from Africa, is standing with its catch. Like other fishing owls, it has no ear tufts. Its talons are sharp and curved to catch slippery fish.

◄ WELL CAUGHT
An osprey kicks up spray as it grabs at a fish swimming just below the surface of the water. Sometimes ospreys take fish as heavy as 2-3 kg – much heavier than their own body weight.

Steller's sea eagle (*Haliaeetus pelagicus*)

▲ FISHY DIET

An African marsh harrier grabs a fish from a river near Natal, South Africa. Most marsh harriers live mainly on amphibians, small mammals, reptiles and insects.

▲ BEST FOOT FORWARD

A Steller's sea eagle extends both legs, talons at the ready, as it swoops down to take a fish. This is the largest of the fishing birds of prey, and it has an exceptionally fearsome bill. It lives around the coasts of the Pacific Ocean in Russia and China, where its favourite food is Pacific salmon. It will also take geese and hares.

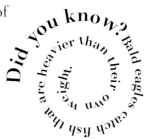

Did you know? Bald eagles catch fish that are heavier than their own weight.

▲ HIGH LOOKOUT

An osprey, or fish hawk, surveys the water below from its untidy treetop nest. This clever fisher supports a number of other birds, such as fish eagles and terns, that rob it of its catch.

▲ AFRICAN ADVENTURES

An African fish eagle goes in for the kill over a lake in central Africa. The eagle pushes its feet forward during the dive and spreads both wings wide to slow the descent. The bird then plucks the unfortunate fish from the surface of the water and returns to feed on a nearby perch.

Focus on

The osprey is outstanding among the fishing birds of prey. Its acceleration is fast and spectacular, beginning high in the air and ending dramatically in the water. Sometimes it will submerge itself completely, unlike other fishing raptors. It feeds in lakes and rivers, and along estuaries and sea coasts. It takes freshwater fish, such as pike and trout. Marine sources of food include herring and flatfish. Although the osprey is a very skilful hunter, not all of its dives are successful. On average, it has to make three or four dives before it succeeds in making a kill. Ospreys may make up to four kills a day to feed themselves, but they need to catch more fish if they are very hungry or when they are feeding chicks in the nest.

1 The osprey soars over the lake, looking for fish swimming close to the water's surface. Once it spots its prey, the osprey falls like a stone out of the sky, gaining speed all the time. It opens out its wings to slow it down seconds before it hits the surface of the water. It brings its feet forwards as it enters the water's surface.

2 The osprey's outstretched feet pierce the surface of the water and thrust towards the fish with open claws. The fish can be nearly a metre down, and the osprey has to plunge right into the water to reach it. This time, however, the fish manages to avoid the hunter's clutches, and the bird looks as if it is taking a bath! In a shower of spray, the osprey struggles back into the air to try again.

Going Fishing

3 The next fish the osprey spies is swimming at the water's surface. Undeterred by the previous failure, the bird judges its dive well, and soon the fish is gripped in the osprey's sharp talons. The spiny surface of the osprey's feet provides extra gripping force and prevents the slippery prey from getting free, no matter how much it wriggles.

4 With powerful beats of its wings, the osprey pulls the fish out of the water. Its feet hold the fish's body head-first to cut down air resistance during the flight.

5 The osprey flies back to its perch. On the way, the bird might get attacked by pirates, birds that harry the osprey and force it to drop its catch, which they then pounce on.

6 With its catch in its claws, the osprey lands on its perch. There it uses its sharp bill to slice through the tough scales and skin of the fish to feast on the tasty flesh.

The Scavengers

Most birds of prey kill prey to eat, but many also scavenge on carrion (dead animals) when they find it. For example, the golden eagle feeds mainly on carrion during winter months, when its usual prey is scarce. However, one group of birds, called vultures, scavenges almost entirely on carrion. Vultures have sharp, sturdy bills for slicing through hides and tearing at meat and sinews. Some have heads, and often their necks, naked of feathers to prevent them becoming caked with blood. Their feet are broad for walking, but weak and with flat claws, because they do not need them to kill. Vultures are noted for their high, soaring flight on long, broad wings. They ride on thermals – warm air currents rising from the ground. They can spot carrion many kilometres away with their excellent eyesight.

▲ AT THE SEASIDE
This Andean condor soars in search of carrion over cliffs on the Pacific coast of South America. Its diet also includes a lot of fish. It has slightly longer wings than the Californian condor, with a wingspan of over 3 m.

▼ BEARDED BONEBREAKER
The lammergeier is also named the bearded vulture due to the black bristles on its face. It is famous for its habit of breaking bones by dropping them on rocks. It eats the bone fragments and the nutritious marrow inside.

Bearded vulture
(*Gypaetus barbatus*)

▲ CRACKING EGGS
An Egyptian vulture uses a stone in its beak to crack the hard shell of an egg. It might be smaller than other vultures, but it seems more intelligent. It is the only tool-user among birds of prey. Ostrich eggs are among its favourite food.

ON PATROL

European griffon vultures soar high in the sky using their long, broad wings. They keep a lookout for signs of carrion down below as they fly. Griffon vultures are common in the mountainous regions of southern Europe and northern Africa, often living in large flocks.

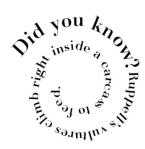

Did you know? Ruppell's vultures climb right inside a carcass to feed.

SUNBATHING

A white-backed vulture stands with its wings wide open, sunning itself in the scorching heat of the African savanna. Many vultures do this, probably to allow their feathers to dry after bathing. They also do this to lose heat through the increased surface area of their spread wings.

COLOURFUL KING

The king vulture has the most colourful and unusual head of all vultures. It is found in Central and South America, where it can be seen soaring over the rainforests and among the high peaks of the Andes mountains in search of carrion.

TUCKING IN

A group of white-backed vultures tucks into the carcass of a freshly killed animal on the plains of Zimbabwe, southern Africa. These vultures soar and wheel high in the sky and are attracted to carrion when they see other vultures gathering around it. With their long, naked necks, they reach deeper inside carcasses to feed than some other vultures.

King vulture
(*Sarcoramphus papa*)

Going Courting

Males and females of most bird species usually get together once a year to mate and produce young. Then as soon as the young birds mature into adults, they too go off to find a mate. Some birds of prey stay with their mate for life. However, courting still takes place every year. This helps strengthen the bond between the two birds. In courtship displays there is usually much calling to each other, with the birds close together. The male may offer the female prey it has caught. Since most birds of prey are superb fliers, however, the most spectacular courtship displays take place in the air. The birds may perform acrobatic dances, or fly side by side, then swoop at each other and even clasp talons. The male may also drop prey whilst in flight for the female to dive and catch in an extravagant game of courtship feeding.

THE MARRIED COUPLE
Like most birds of prey, American bald eagles usually mate for life. They occupy the same nest year after year, gradually adding to it each time they return to breed.

TOGETHERNESS
Secretary birds become inseparable for life once they have paired up. Their courtship flights are most impressive, as they fly through the sky with their long tails streaming behind them. The birds also sleep side by side in their nest. They use their nests as living quarters throughout the year, not just during the breeding season.

BEARING GIFTS

A male barn owl has caught a mouse and presents it to his mate back in the nest. This behaviour is called courtship feeding. It helps strengthen the bond between the pair. It is also preparation for the time when the male will have to feed the female when she is nest-bound and incubating their eggs.

BALANCING ACT

A pair of ospreys struggle to keep their balance as they mate on a high perch. While the female turns her tail to one side, the male lowers his tail and presses his cloaca (sexual organ) against hers. His sperm can then be transferred to her body, and she can lay fertilized eggs that will hatch into chicks.

Did you know? Peregrines spend hours performing an amazing courtship flight.

CARACARAS ON DISPLAY

A pair of striated caracaras call to one another by their nest. They are no longer courting but raising young. Mated pairs display like this frequently to strengthen the bond between them. Caracaras can raise two broods (groups of chicks hatched together) a year in South America, but in Florida, they are usually single-brooded.

Osprey
(*Pandion haliaetus*)

FACE TO FACE

A pair of Egyptian vultures stand face to face on the ground in an elaborate courtship display. In addition to their ground-based display, the pair also perform spectacular aerial displays. They fly, climb and dive close together, often presenting each other their talons.

Building Nests and Laying Eggs

Courtship displays help the male and female birds to bond. They also help establish the pair's territory, the area in which they hunt. Within this territory, the birds build a nest in which the female lays her eggs. Birds of prey usually nest far apart, because they need a large hunting area. However, some species, including griffon vultures and lesser kestrels, nest in colonies. Birds of prey choose many different nesting sites, in caves and on cliffs, in barns and the disused nests of other birds, on the ground or high up in trees. The nests themselves may be simple scrapes on a ledge, no more than a bare place for the eggs to rest in. Other nests are elaborate structures built of branches and twigs. Many birds return to the same nest with the same mate every year, adding to it until it becomes a massive structure.

CAMOUFLAGE COLOURS

This hen harrier is nesting on the ground among vegetation. The female, pictured brooding (sitting on her eggs), has the typical mottled-brown plumage of ground-nesting birds. This makes her hard to spot on the nest. The male often feeds the female in the air. He calls her to him, then drops the prey for her to catch.

Bonelli's eagle
(*Hieraaetus fasciatus*)

SETTING UP HOME

A female Bonelli's eagle repairs her clifftop, keeping a careful watch over her young chick. If there are no cliffs in her territory, the female will build her nest at the top of a tall tree. The nests measure just under 2 m in diameter, and they are used year after year. You can see that scientists have ringed this chick's leg.

▶ GO AWAY!

With its wings spread wide to make it look bigger, a barn owl adopts a threatening pose to protect his nest. The female has already laid several eggs, which she will incubate for just over a month. During this time, the male feeds her, usually with rats, mice or voles, but sometimes with insects and small birds. If food is plentiful, the pair may raise two broods a year.

◀ IN A SCRAPE

On a cliff ledge, this peregrine falcon has made a simple nest called a scrape, clearing a small patch of ground to nest on. Many peregrines use traditional nesting sites, where birds have made their homes for centuries. Others have adapted to life in the city, making their scrapes on the ledges of skyscrapers, office buildings and churches.

◀ FULL UP

A secretary bird comes in to land on the huge tree-top nest of a colony of social weaver birds in search of its own nesting site. As this tree is full, the bird will have to choose another site in which to nest. It prefers low thorny trees such as the acacia. It makes its nest out of sticks, lining it with soft grass.

Secretary bird
(*Sagittarius serpentarius*)

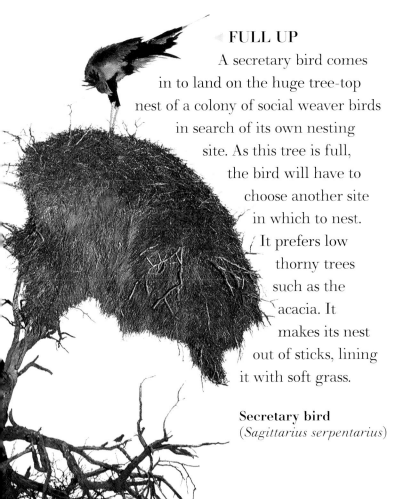

▲ SECOND-HAND

A disused raven's nest has been adopted by this peregrine falcon. Peregrines do not build their own nest but often lay eggs in nests abandoned by other birds. The eggs are incubated by both parents. Falcon eggs are pale reddish-brown, unlike those of most other raptors, which are white or speckled.

103

Focus on

Once a pair of birds has mated the female lays her eggs. The number of eggs laid depends on the species. Large raptors, such as eagles, lay one or two eggs. Smaller raptors, such as kestrels, may lay up to 8 eggs. The eggs have to be incubated (kept warm) after they have been laid so that the baby birds can develop inside. This is done by one of the birds brooding (sitting on the eggs) in the nest all the time. Brooding is done usually by the female. The male's job is to bring the female food. Incubation times vary widely, from less than a month for small falcons to nearly two months for eagles and vultures.

1 A young Mauritius kestrel chick develops inside its egg, feeding on the nutrients surrounding it. Once the chick has grown enough, it begins to chip away at the shell with a projection on its bill called an egg tooth. In time, it makes a little hole, called a pip.

2 Pipping puts the chick in touch with the outside world, and its lungs breathe in the outside air. The chick rests for several hours and then starts hammering away with its egg tooth next to the first pip. After a while the chick twists around and starts hammering again. It does this until it has chipped right round the shell.

3 With the shell cracked, the chick starts its fight to break out. It presses its feet against the lower part of the shell and heaves with its shoulders against the upper part. Soon the top of the egg breaks off, and the head of the chick becomes visible.

Hatching Out

4 The chick kicks and heaves as it continues its fight to escape from the shell, resting frequently to regain its strength. Soon its head is free, then a wing and finally a leg. The chick prepares itself for a last push.

5 With all its remaining strength, the chick forces its body away from the shell. It lies almost motionless, wet and nearly naked, weak and helpless. The chick will need to rest for several hours before it has the strength to beg for food. This can be a dangerous time for the chick. It might be trampled by clumsy parents.

6 When the newly hatched chick dries out, its body is covered with sparse, fluffy down. This early down is not enough to keep the chick warm, so it has to snuggle up to its mother in the nest. Gradually, a thicker cover of down grows, which can be seen on these two-week-old kestrel chicks. A full covering of downy feathers will keep them warm and allow their mother to leave the nest.

A Chick's Life

When chicks hatch out, they find it difficult to move. They are unable to stand, and just sit on their ankles. Their bodies are covered with fine down, which cannot keep them warm. So they need their mother's warmth to stay alive. That is why she still does not move from the nest. The male continues to bring food, which she tears and feeds to the chicks. After a couple of weeks, a thicker down grows on the chicks' bodies to keep them warm, and the female can leave the nest and go hunting again. Soon the chicks grow strong enough to stand up and move about. In species where the eggs hatch at different times, older chicks beg the most food and grow strongest. This can result in the death of the weaker chicks.

CHICK AND RAT
A barn owl chick is feeding on a rat its parents have caught. The chick is about six weeks old, and already the well-defined face patch characteristic of all owls has begun to appear.

SITTING PRETTY
A secretary bird and its chick rest in their nest in a thorny tree on the African savanna. First, the parents feed the chick on regurgitated liquids. Later, they regurgitate rodents, insects and snakes into the nest for the chick to eat. The chick is fully feathered in five weeks and stays in the nest for about a month longer.

FEEDING TIME

In its nest high up in a tall tree, a female booted eagle feeds its chick. The chick is several weeks old and still covered in thick down, but its feathers are beginning to appear. Both parents feed the chick, often hunting the same prey together. The booted eagle is one of the smallest eagles, with its body measuring about 50 cm from head to tail.

LEMMING FEAST

A lemming is the next meal for this snowy owl chick. Lemmings are the staple (usual) diet of this owl. When lemmings are in plentiful supply, snowy owls may raise as many as eight chicks at a time. The eggs are laid over a considerable period of time, so there is a noticeable size difference between the young owls in large clutches.

Snowy owl (*Nyctea scandiaca*)

THREE IN A HOLE

Three kestrel chicks peer out of their nest in a hole in a tree. By the time they are a month old, they will have left the nest and be flying. It will take them up to another five weeks to copy their parents and master the art of hovering in the air to scan for prey.

Raising the Young

Young birds of prey remain in the nest for different periods, depending on the species. The young of smaller birds, such as merlins, are nest-bound for only about eight weeks. The young of larger species, such as the golden eagle, stay in the nest for more than three months. Young vultures may stay for over five months. As the chicks grow, their thick down moults to reveal their proper feathers. They become stronger and start to exercise their wings by standing up and flapping them. Shortly before they leave the nest, they make their first flight. This greatest step in the life of a young bird is called fledging. It takes weeks or even months before the fledglings (trainee fliers) have learned the flying and hunting skills they need to catch prey. During this time, they are still dependent on their parents for all their food.

▲ **TAKING OFF**

A young kestrel launches itself into the air. It is fully grown but still has its juvenile plumage. Other adults recognize the plumage, so they do not drive the young bird away.

▼ **GROWING UP**

The pictures below show three stages in the early life of a tawny owl. At four weeks, the chick is a fluffy ball of down. At seven weeks, it is quite well feathered. At 12 weeks, it is fully feathered and can fly.

4 weeks old

7 weeks old

12 weeks old

Pygmy falcon adult

Pygmy falcon juvenile
(*Poliohierax
semitorquatus*)

BIG PYGMY

This pygmy falcon parent is still feeding its chick, which is as big as the parent is. In the early stages of the chick's life, the male pygmy falcon supplies all the food, while the female keeps the chick warm in the nest. Then both adults feed the fledgling, until the young bird learns to catch insects for itself. This skill can take up to two months to master.

MONTH-OLD KESTREL CHICKS

Two young kestrels huddle together near their nest in an old farm building. They are fully feathered and almost ready to take their first flight. However, it could be another month before they learn to hunt.

JUST PRACTISING

This tawny owl is still unable to fly. It is flapping its wings up and down to exercise and strengthen the pectoral (chest) muscles that will enable it to fly. As these muscles get stronger, the young bird will sometimes lift off its perch. Eventually, often on a windy day, the owl will find itself flying in the air. On this first flight, it will not travel far. Within days, it will be flying just like its parents.

Tawny owl
(*Strix aluco*)

Open Country

Birds of prey are found almost everywhere in the world. However, each species prefers a different kind of habitat, in which it can hunt certain kinds of prey. This prevents too much competition for the food resources available. Many species prefer open country habitats. Imperial and golden eagles hunt in open mountainous country. On the bleak expanses of the Arctic tundra the gyrfalcon and snowy owl are the most successful predators. The vast savanna lands of eastern and southern Africa are the home of many vultures. Here, there are rich pickings on the carcasses of grazing animals killed by big cats such as the cheetah and lion. Areas where farming is practised are common hunting grounds for kestrels and harriers.

▲ GROUND NESTER
A young Montagu's harrier spreads its wings in the nest. Like other harriers, it nests among thick vegetation. This harrier lives on open moors and farmland throughout Europe, northern Africa and Asia.

Did you know? The gyrfalcon is the largest falcon, up to 62 cm from head to tail.

◀ TUNDRA HUNTER
A gyrfalcon devours its prey. This bird lives in the cold, wide-open spaces of the Arctic tundra, in Alaska, northern Canada and northern Europe. The bird in the picture is a young bird with dark, juvenile plumage. The adult is much paler – grey above and white underneath. Some birds are almost pure white and blend in perfectly with their snowy habitat.

VULTURES AT THE CAPE

The Cape vultures of southern Africa inhabit the clifftops and hilly regions around the Cape of Good Hope. They have broad wings that enable them to soar effortlessly on the warm air currents rising from the hot land below. Often, several birds soar together, watching out for a meal to share and guarding their territory against other vultures.

KILLING FIELDS

A common buzzard feeds on carrion—a dead rabbit that it has recently found. Buzzards, or buteos, are found in open and lightly wooded country throughout the world. They live in both lowland and highland areas and feed mainly on small mammals.

PLAINS WALKER

The secretary bird can be found in most savanna, or grassland, habitats in Africa south of the Sahara desert. Its long legs enable it to walk through all but the tallest grass. It avoids forests, but it does build its nest in trees.

SUNNING ON THE SAVANNA

A juvenile bateleur eagle suns itself on a tree in the sparse savanna (open plains) of Africa, keeping a watchful eye for small mammals and reptiles. It takes six years for a juvenile to reach full maturity.

Bateleur eagle
(*Terathopius ecaudatus*)

111

Woodlands and Wetlands

Honey buzzard (*Pernis apivorus*)

▲ **FOREST FEEDER**

The honey buzzard is commonly found in the deciduous forests of Europe, where it feeds mainly on the larvae of bees and wasps. It is quite a small bird, with a delicate bill suited to its diet.

The world's woodlands make good hunting grounds for many different birds of prey. The sparrowhawk and goshawk, and the common and honey buzzards, all make their homes in woodland habitats. Many owls prefer a wooded habitat, nesting in both coniferous and broad-leafed trees. The most formidable forest predators, however, are the enormous South American harpy eagle and the Philippine eagle. They live in rainforests and hunt monkey prey high in the treetops. Freshwater and marine wetlands are the territory of the sea and fishing eagles and the osprey. Among the smaller birds of prey, peregrines hunt around sea cliffs, while marsh harriers hunt among the reed beds of freshwater marshes. In Africa and Asia, the fishing owls make their homes in woodlands close to the coast or by inland waterways.

◄ **IN THE MARSHES**

Three marsh harrier chicks peep out of their reed nest in a swampy region of Poland. Marsh harriers are the largest harriers, measuring up to 55 cm from head to tail. They hunt in the reed beds and on open farmland nearby. These fearsome hunters will eat most birds, small mammals, reptiles, and amphibians.

◄ DOWN IN THE JUNGLE

The harpy eagle lives in the thick forests and jungles of Central and South America. It is an awesome predator, picking animals as big as sloths and monkeys from the trees, as well as birds such as parrots. Harpy eagles grow up to a metre from head to tail. They have huge talons to grip their heavy prey.

▲ DAYLIGHT OWL

A hawk owl perches on a tree stump. The hawk owl lives in the massive conifer forests of northern Canada and Alaska. It can often be seen in daylight.

▼ EAGLE AT SEA

This white-bellied sea eagle lives high on the clifftops of an island in Indonesia, South-east Asia. Like other sea eagles, it takes fish from both coastal and inland waters and also feeds on carrion. This bird will also eat poisonous sea snakes.

▲ FLEET FLIER

The sparrowhawk is found in the woodlands of Europe and Asia. It flies swiftly and close to the ground, using the dense vegetation as cover. However, it sometimes hunts like a peregrine, circling high and then diving steeply at its prey.

On the Move

Every bird of prey maintains a territory in which it can feed and breed. There is usually no room for the parents' offspring, so they have to forge a new territory themselves. The parents may stay in their breeding area all year long if there is enough food. If not, they may migrate (move away) to somewhere warmer in winter, sometimes because their prey have themselves migrated. For example, peregrines that bred on the tundra in northern Europe fly some 14,000 kilometres to spend winter in South Africa.

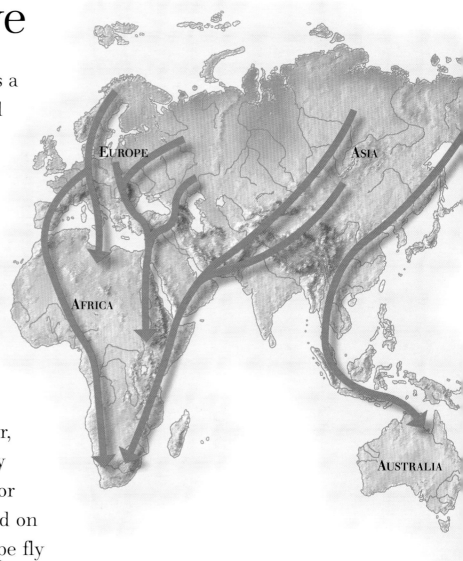

EUROPE ASIA AFRICA AUSTRALIA

◁ ESCAPING SOUTH
The rough-legged buzzard is slightly larger than its cousin, the common buzzard. It breeds in far northern regions of the world in the spring, both on the treeless tundra and the forested taiga. In the autumn, it migrates south to escape the cold Arctic winter.

▲ FLIGHT PATHS
Birds avoid migrating over large stretches of water. There are fewer uplifting air currents over water than there are over land. So many migration routes pass through regions where there is a convenient land bridge or a short sea crossing. Panama, in Central America, is one such area. Gibraltar, in southern Europe, is another.

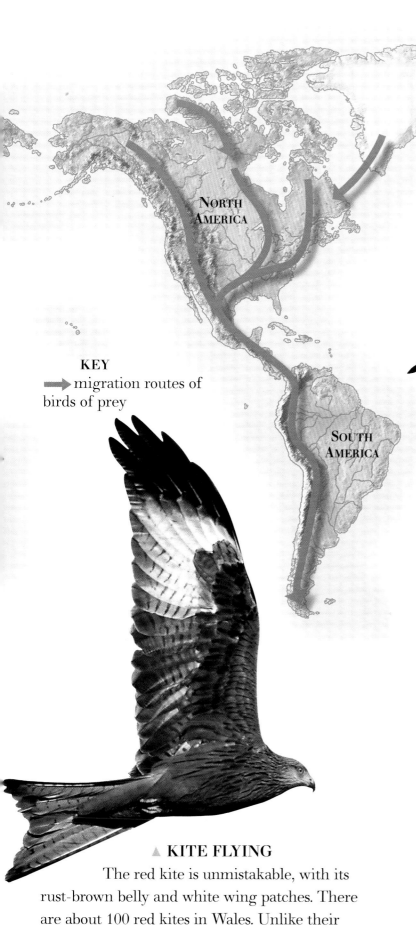

KEY
→ migration routes of birds of prey

NORTH AMERICA

SOUTH AMERICA

▼ JUST PASSING

This sooty falcon was spotted on its way south to the island of Madagascar, where it spends the winter. In spring, it will return to northeast Africa or Israel to breed.

Sooty falcon
(*Falco concolor*)

▲ KITE FLYING

The red kite is unmistakable, with its rust-brown belly and white wing patches. There are about 100 red kites in Wales. Unlike their continental European cousins, those that breed in Wales do not usually migrate south in winter.

▲ GRACEFUL FLOCK

Graceful kites fly over an Indian village during their annual migration from Asia to warmer winter quarters in southern Africa. They will cover hundreds of kilometres a day.

115

Orders and Families

▲ NIGHT-HUNTERS

This great grey owl is one of about 130 species of owls. Most, but not all, are nocturnal (night) hunters. Owls belong to the order Strigiformes and are not related to the other birds of prey.

There are more than 400 species of birds of prey. Each is different in size, colouring, behaviour and feeding pattern from every other species. Birds of prey fall into two major groupings, or orders. The diurnal raptors, the day-time hunters, belong to the order Falconiformes. The owls, the night-hunters, belong to the order Strigiformes. Within each order, similar kinds of birds are classed together in family groups. In the Falconiformes, there are five families. The secretary bird and the osprey have a family each. New World vultures form another family, and the falcons and caracaras another. But by far the largest family, containing more than 200 species, is the so-called accipiters, which include eagles, Old World vultures, kites, hawks and buzzards.

Roman Eagle

To the ancient Romans, the eagle symbolized power, nobility, strength and courage. When the Roman army marched into battle, one soldier at the head of each legion (group of soldiers) carried a golden eagle on a standard (see left). The Roman name for the eagle was aquila. Today, this name is given to a family of eagles, including the magnificent golden eagle.

▶ THE CARACARAS

This striated caracara lives in the Falkland Islands. It is the member of a group within the falcon family. Caracaras are large, long-legged birds found from the southern United States to southern South America. Unlike true falcons, they often hunt on the ground.

ALL ALONE

There is only one species of osprey the world over. This one is nesting in Maryland, in the eastern USA, where it is known as a fish hawk. Some of the largest colonies of ospreys are found in north-eastern Africa.

TALL SECRETARY

The secretary bird looks like no other bird of prey, so it is not surprising that it has a family all to itself. Its distinctive features are a crest on its head, very long tail and legs, and short, stubby toes.

OLD WORLD VULTURES

These white-backed vultures live in southern Africa. They belong to a family of some 14 species of vultures, found in the "Old World", that is, Europe, Asia and Africa. Like all vultures, they live largely on carrion, often the remains of prey killed by big cats like lions.

King vulture
(*Sarcoramphus papa*)

VULTURES OF THE NEW WORLD

The king vulture displays its impressive 1.7-metre wingspan. This bird is the most colourful and maybe the most handsome vulture of all. It is one of the seven species of "New World" vultures, found in the Americas. The Andean and Californian condors are two other members of this group.

White-backed vulture
(*Gyps africanus*)

117

Focus on

Most eagles are very large, aggressive birds, preying on both small and large mammals, other birds and reptiles. Although some are hardly bigger than buzzards, they are in general fiercer and more active. Each eagle has a different lifestyle and hunting strategy. The golden eagle swoops down from on high mostly on mammal prey. The bald eagle takes mainly fish. The tawny eagle will eat anything. The most distinctive feature of the bateleur eagle is its acrobatic manoeuvres in the air. Its name comes from a French word meaning acrobat.

FAMILY LIFE

A bald eagle returns to its nest with a rock ptarmigan in its talons. Now it will tear strips of meat from its prey and feed them to its two offspring. These two eaglets are only a few weeks old and have just grown their thick second coat of down. They are still not strong enough to stand on their legs.

Bateleur eagle (juvenile)
(*Terathopius ecaudata*)

YOUNG AND OLD

For the first few years of its life, the bateleur eagle has drab brown juvenile plumage (*left*). But by the sixth year, it has acquired glorious adult plumage (*right*), which signals that it is now mature and ready to breed.

Bateleur eagle (adult)

Eagles

MARTIAL LORE

A martial eagle swoops down from the skies to deliver a deadly blow to a monitor lizard basking in the searing-hot African savanna. This heavy bird, with its huge wingspan of up to 2.5 m, will often capture small animals, mostly reptiles, but it usually feeds on game birds. The martial eagle is persecuted by humans because it occasionally attacks domestic livestock such as chickens and goats.

TAWNY SCAVENGER

The tawny eagle of Africa is mainly a scavenger. It often joins a flock of vultures to feed on the carcasses of prey killed by big cats, such as the zebra in this photograph. It also frequently steals prey from other raptors.

Golden eagle
(*Aquila chrysaetos*)

MASTER OF THE MOUNTAINS

A golden eagle opens its wings wide. They span nearly 2.5 m. This magnificent bird gets its name from the golden tinges on its head and neck feathers. It lives in remote mountains around the world and feeds on birds, mammals and carrion.

Fellow Hunters

Birds of prey are probably the most feared hunters of the bird world. However, they are not the only birds that hunt live prey. Other birds catch insects and worms, amphibians and fish, and even small mammals and other birds. Most common are the insect-eaters, such as the bee-eater and the flycatcher. Wading birds, such as the oystercatcher, feed on worms and crustaceans, while herons eat amphibians and fish. Skimmers, pelicans and all kinds of seabirds live mainly on fish. Many seabirds prey on the chicks of other species, as do magpies on land. Many birds, especially those belonging to the crow family, will eat small mammals and carrion. However, none of these birds is classed as a bird of prey, for they lack the formidable sharp, hooked bill and lethal, taloned feet of the raptor.

Kookaburra
(*Dacelo gigas*)

▲ KOOKABURRA CATCH

A snake makes a good meal for this Australian kookaburra. It eats more or less anything, from frogs to small mammals and other small birds.

▲ BIG BILL

The turkey-sized African ground hornbill loves to eat snakes, even very poisonous ones such as cobras. It kills them by repeatedly squeezing up and down their bodies with the tip of its large, powerful bill.

▼ HUNTER-SCAVENGER

A harvest mouse has just been killed by this common crow. The crow will also eat insects and the eggs and young of other birds, as well as carrion. Other members of the crow family, such as jackdaws and magpies, have a similar diet.

Crow
(*Corvus corone*)

STANDING IN WAIT

The great blue heron of North America stands absolutely still at the water's edge, scanning the water for fish as they swim by. When it sees a fish, the heron thrusts its long bill into the water lightning-fast and grabs it with deadly accuracy. It hits the fish on the ground to kill it, before swallowing it head-first. Herons also eat frogs and mammals such as voles.

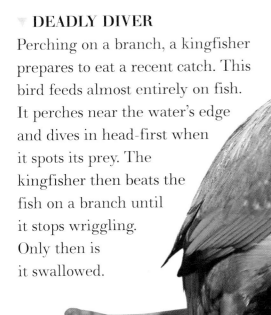

BROWN BULLY

A brown skua swoops down to take a giant petrel chick on the remote Atlantic island of South Georgia. Skuas are always on the lookout for eggs and chicks left in nests whilst the parent birds are away feeding. They are also known for harrying (chasing) birds that have just been fishing. They make them disgorge (throw up) their food and eat it themselves.

Did you know? Butcher birds impale their prey on sharp thorns.

DEADLY DIVER

Perching on a branch, a kingfisher prepares to eat a recent catch. This bird feeds almost entirely on fish. It perches near the water's edge and dives in head-first when it spots its prey. The kingfisher then beats the fish on a branch until it stops wriggling. Only then is it swallowed.

Kingfisher
(*Alcedo atthis*)

121

Hood

Perch

Falconry

Hunting with birds of prey is called falconry or hawking. It has been a popular sport in the Middle East for thousands of years. Today it has many followers in other parts of the world. Falconers use a variety of birds for hunting. Some prefer to use true falcons, or longwings, such as peregrines. However, shortwings, such as goshawks, and the broadwings, such as buzzards, are also used. Falconers need skill and patience to train a bird. First they must gain the bird's trust so that it will sit and feed on the fist. This process is known as manning. Then the bird must be trained to get fit and to learn to chase prey. Falconers fly birds on long lines, called creances, before allowing them to fly free. Other special equipment used in falconry includes jesses (leg fastenings), hoods (blindfolds) and lures (imitation prey).

▲ **IN THE DARK**
This picture displays two essential features of falconry equipment, or furniture. The leather hood is used when the bird is on the perch and also when it is taken out hunting. Falcons such as the one above need a flat block perch to rest on.

▶ **ARAB SPORT**
An Arab falconer proudly displays a falcon as it perches on a strong leather glove on his fist. Falconry has been a popular sport in the Middle East ever since it began there more than 3,000 years ago. The favourite birds of Arab falconers are the saker and the peregrine falcon.

122

▶ KITTED OUT

A lanner falcon is about to fly back to its handler. A leash is threaded through a ring (swivel) on the jess, which is attached to the leg of the falcon. A bell helps the falconer to locate the bird if it wanders.

Bell

Jess

▲ LURING AND STOOPING

Moving at speed, a lanner falcon chases a lure being swung by a falconer. Falconers use lures to get falcons fit and agile and teach them to be persistent hunters. They swing the lure around their bodies or high in the air, tempting the bird to fly at it and stoop (dive swiftly).

Did you know? A hawk's bent flight feathers can be straightened by steaming.

▲ ON THE FIST

The first stage in training a bird is to get it to sit on the fist whilst tethered. When it first does so, the bird should be rewarded with a piece of meat. Soon, the bird should actively step up, then jump on the fist to feed.

▲ HAROLD GOES HAWKING

In a scene on the famous Bayeux tapestry, King Harold of England is seen riding with a hawk on his fist. The tapestry portrays events leading up to the Battle of Hastings and the conquest of England by the Normans in 1066. Hawking, or falconry, was a favourite sport of noblemen in the Middle Ages.

Under Threat

In the wild, birds of prey have few natural enemies except, perhaps, other birds of prey. In many habitats they are the top predator. They have only one thing to fear – humans. Over the centuries, people have hunted raptors as vermin (pests) because they have occasionally killed domestic livestock, such as birds raised for game. Recently humans have been killing birds of prey indirectly by using pesticides on seeds and crops. When birds catch contaminated animals, pesticides build up in their own bodies and eventually poison them, causing death. Many birds of prey are now protected by law. This, and the safer use of farm chemicals, has led to a recovery in the numbers of several species. However, the indiscriminate shooting of migrating birds is still a threat, as is the destruction of forest habitats in which they live.

TRIGGER HAPPY

A shooting enthusiast takes aim. A dog stands nearby, ready to retrieve the fallen bird. Raptors are shot by irresponsible hunters every year, especially as they flock together when migrating.

GRIM WARNING

A dead hawk is left dangling on a piece of rope. This age-old practice is used by gamekeepers and farmers to warn off other birds of prey or vermin (pests) such as crows.

PHILIPPINE EAGLE

The Philippine eagle is one of the rarest of all birds of prey. This is because the dense tropical forest in which it lives is rapidly being destroyed for farming and for humans to live. The eagle gets its name from the Philippine Islands, in Southeast Asia, where it lives. It eats mammals called lemurs, various kinds of birds and sometimes monkeys.

DEADLY CHEMICALS

A sparrowhawk has been poisoned to death. It has preyed on smaller birds that have eaten seeds or insects sprayed with chemical pesticides. Gradually, the chemicals built up in the sparrowhawk's body until they made it ill, finally causing its death.

Did you know? Barn owls and kites are killed by eating poison-resistant rats.

Alice and the Griffin
A griffin sits next to Alice in a scene from Alice's Adventures in Wonderland. *The griffin is a mythical bird. According to Greek legend, it had the head and wings of an eagle but the body of a lion.*

HIT AND RUN

A barn owl lies dead at the roadside, battered by a passing vehicle the night before. Motor vehicles kill thousands of birds every day and every night. At night, owls often hunt for small prey, such as mice and voles, in roadside verges and hedges. Their habit of slow-flying close to the ground puts them in danger from passing cars and trucks.

Conservation

Conservationists aim to protect species of animals and birds that are in danger of extinction. They study the habitats, lifestyles and movements of birds of prey by catching them, putting rings around their legs and tracking their movements. They have also preserved many species that were on the brink of extinction by breeding them in captivity, then releasing the offspring back into the wild. Today there are study centres and sanctuaries worldwide, where birds of prey can be closely observed. Here the public also has the chance to see them in action. The future of many species of birds of prey is more secure in parts of the world where there is a "greener" approach to wildlife and the environment.

▲ UP THE POLE
Some birds prefer human-made structures to trees when it comes to nesting. In Glacier National Park, fake telephone posts were built for ospreys to nest on when experts found that nests on real posts caused line interference.

◀ THE RAREST
The Californian condor is the rarest of all birds of prey. It became extinct in the wild in the 1980s. The last few birds were taken into captivity, where they fortunately began to breed. Several pairs of Californian condors have already been released successfully back into the wild.

Californian condor
(Gymnogyps californianus)

▲ FLYING LESSONS
In 1998, firefighters abseiled down a 91 m cliff to rescue a three-month-old falcon. The fledgling's leg had become entangled in barbed wire. After being treated by a local vet, the falcon was taught to hunt and fly at a bird of prey centre in Newent, England, before being released back into the wild.

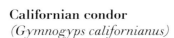

ON THE LOOKOUT

Bird-watchers gather in the Everglades National Park in Florida, USA. This outstanding wetland habitat is now a conservation area. Visitors can spot many birds of prey, including America's national bird, the bald eagle.

THE EAGLE'S RINGS

Bird-watchers put a ring on the leg of a Bonelli's eagle. The team have already measured, sexed and weighed the bird, and recorded where it was captured. The bird is released when all the recordings are taken. If it is caught again another year, the bird's condition and location can be compared to these records, helping to keep a check on the health and movements of the eagle population.

Did you know? Peregrines are no longer endangered in North America.

HANDLE WITH CARE

Here in a Kenyan wildlife park, a bird handler is showing off a Crowned Eagle. Sanctuaries for birds of prey have been set up in many countries across the world. Visitors are often treated to spectacular flying displays by diverse raptors.

CROCODILES

Cold-blooded crocodilians have been around for thousands of years, and are the largest reptiles today. Their awesome jaws are designed for gripping, crushing and teasing the flesh off their prey. Yet there's nothing a crocodile enjoys more than eating, basking and mating in the company of friends.

Author: Barbara Taylor
Consultant: Dr. Richard A. Griffiths,
Durrell Institute of
Conservation and Ecology

What is a Crocodilian?

Crocodilians are scaly, armour-clad reptiles that include crocodiles, alligators, caimans and gharials. They are survivors from a prehistoric age – their relatives first lived on Earth with the dinosaurs nearly 200 million years ago. Today, they are the dinosaurs' closest living relatives, apart from birds.

Crocodilians are fierce predators. They lurk motionless in rivers, lakes and swamps, waiting to snap up prey with their enormous jaws and tough teeth. Their prey ranges from insects, frogs and fish to birds and large mammals, such as deer and zebras. Very few crocodilians regularly attack and kill humans. Most are timid. Crocodilians usually live in warm, tropical places in or near freshwater, and some live in the sea. They hunt and feed mainly in the water, but crawl on to dry land to sunbathe, nest and lay their eggs.

▲ SCALY TAILS
Like many crocodilians, an American alligator uses its long, strong tail to swim through the water. The tail moves from side to side to push the alligator along. The tail is the same length as the rest of the body.

Long, strong tail has flat sides to push aside water for swimming.

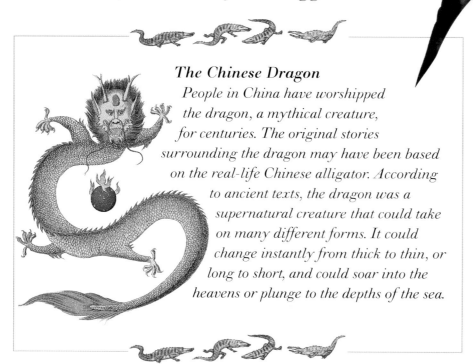

The Chinese Dragon
People in China have worshipped the dragon, a mythical creature, for centuries. The original stories surrounding the dragon may have been based on the real-life Chinese alligator. According to ancient texts, the dragon was a supernatural creature that could take on many different forms. It could change instantly from thick to thin, or long to short, and could soar into the heavens or plunge to the depths of the sea.

▶ CROCODILIAN CHARACTERISTICS
With its thick, scaly skin, huge jaws and powerful tail, this American alligator looks like a living dinosaur. Its eyes and nostrils are on top of the head so that it can see and breathe when the rest of its body is underwater. On land, crocodilians slither along on their bellies, but they can lift themselves up on their four short legs to walk.

▲ TALKING HEADS

Huge, powerful jaws lined with sharp teeth make Nile crocodiles killing machines. They are some of the world's largest and most dangerous reptiles. The teeth are used to attack and grip prey, but are no good for chewing. Prey has to be swallowed whole or in chunks.

► SHUT EYE

Although this spectacled caiman has its eyes shut, it is probably not asleep, but dozing. Scientists think that crocodilians just catnap rather than sleeping deeply as humans do. Two butterflies have landed on the caiman's eye and nose, perhaps in search of salty moisture.

► SOAKING UP THE SUN

Nile crocodiles sun themselves on a sandbank. This is called basking and warms the body. Crocodilians are cold-blooded, which means that their body temperature is affected by their surroundings. They have no fur or feathers to keep them warm, nor can they shiver to warm up. They move in and out of the water to warm up or cool down.

The scales on the back are usually much more bony than those on the belly.

Scaly skin covers the whole body for protection and camouflage.

Did you know? Most crocodilians live for about 50 years but some live up to 100.

Eyes and nostrils on top of the head.

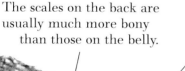

The digits (toes) of each foot are slightly webbed.

American alligator (*Alligator mississippiensis*)

Long snout with sharp teeth to catch prey.

131

Croc or Gator?

There are 13 species (kinds) of crocodile; two species of alligator, six species of caimans; and two species of gharial. Gharials have distinctive long, slender snouts, but crocodiles and alligators are often more difficult to tell apart. Crocodiles usually have longer, more pointed snouts than alligators. Crocodiles also have one very large tooth sticking up from each side of the bottom jaw when they close their mouths.

▲ **CAIMAN EYES**

Most caimans have bonier ridges between their eyes than alligators. These ridges help strengthen the skull and look like the spectacles people wear to help them see. Caimans are usually smaller than alligators.

Chinese alligator
(*Alligator sinensis*)

▲ **COOL ALLIGATOR**

There are two species of alligator, the Chinese alligator (*shown above*) and the American alligator. Alligators are the only crocodilians that can survive cooler temperatures and live outside the tropics.

GREENLAND

EUROPE

NORTH AMERICA

Atlantic Ocean

ASIA

Pacific Ocean

KEY
AFRICA

■ crocodiles

SOUTH AMERICA

Indian Ocean

■ alligators/ caimans

AUSTRALIA

■ gharials

▲ **WHERE IN THE WORLD?**

Crocodiles are the most widespread crocodilian and live in Central and South America, Africa, southern Asia and Australia. Caimans live in Central and South America, while alligators live in the south-eastern USA and China. The gharial is found in southern Asia, while the false gharial lives in South-east Asia.

▼ **A CROCODILE'S SMILE**

With its mouth closed, a crocodile's fourth tooth in the lower jaw fits into a notch on the outside of the upper jaw. No teeth can be seen on the bottom jaw of an alligator's closed mouth.

▶ DIFFERENT SNOUTS

Crocodilian snouts are different shapes and sizes because of the food they eat and the way they live. Gharials and crocodiles have narrow, pointy snouts suited to eating fish. Alligators and caimans have wider, rounder snouts which can manage larger prey, such as birds and mammals. Their jaws are strong enough to overpower victims that are even larger than they are.

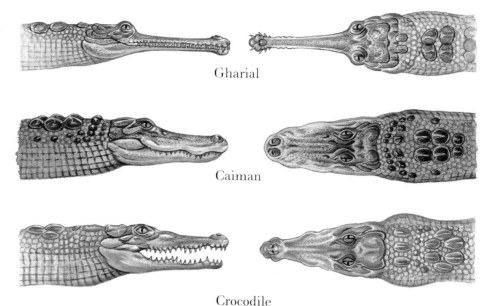

Gharial

Caiman

Crocodile

◀ OUT TO SEA

The enormous saltwater crocodile, often called the saltie, has the largest range of all the crocodilians. It is found from the east coast of India through South-east Asia to the Philippines, New Guinea and northern Australia. Saltwater crocodiles are one of the few species found far out to sea, but they do live in freshwater rivers and lakes as well.

▶ POT NOSE

Two species of gharial, the gharial, or gavial, and the false gharial, live in the rivers, lakes and swamps of southern Asia. The name comes from the knob on the nose of the male gharial, which is called a ghara (pot) in the Hindi language. Some experts say the false gharial is a species of crocodile and is therefore not really part of the gharial family.

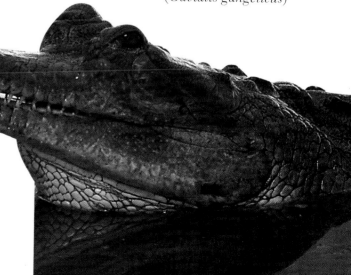

Adult male gharials have a conspicuous knob at the tip of their snouts.

Gharial
(*Gavialis gangeticus*)

Large and Small

Can you imagine a crocodile that weighs as much as three cars? A big, 7m-long saltwater crocodile is as heavy as this. It is the heaviest living reptile in the world. Other enormous crocodilians include Nile crocodiles, gharials and American alligators, which can reach lengths of 5.5m or more. Very large crocodiles and alligators are now rare because many are hunted and killed for their meat and skins before they grow to their maximum size. The smallest species of crocodilian are the dwarf caimans of South America and the African dwarf crocodile. These forest-dwelling reptiles grow to about 1.5m long.

▲ **BIGGEST CAIMAN**
The black caiman is the largest of the caimans. It can grow to over 6m long and is the biggest predator in South America. Black caimans live in the flooded Amazon forest, around lakes and slow-flowing rivers. They hunt at night for capybara, turtles, deer and fish.

▲ **A CROC IN THE HAND**
A person holds a baby Orinoco crocodile (*top*) and a baby spectacled caiman (*bottom*). As adults, the Orinoco crocodile will be twice the length of the caiman, reaching about 5m. You can clearly see how the crocodile has a longer, thinner snout than the caiman.

Crocodile God
The ancient Egyptians worshiped the crocodile-headed god Sebek. He was the god of lakes and rivers, and is shown here with Pharaoh Amenhotep III. A shrine to Sebek was built at Shedet. Here, a Nile crocodile decorated with gold rings and bracelets lived in a special pool. It was believed to be the living god. Other crocodiles were also treated with great respect and hand-fed on meat, cakes, milk and honey.

◄ SUPER-SNOUTED CROCODILE

The mugger crocodile of India and surrounding lands has the broadest snout of all crocodiles, making it look more like an alligator. Adult males reach about 4m long. The name mugger comes from its habit of snatching fish out of people's fishing nets.

◄ SMALLEST CROCODILIAN

Cuvier's dwarf caiman is about a fifth of the size of a giant saltwater crocodile, yet it would still only just fit on your bed! It lives in the rainforests of the Amazon basin in South America. It has particularly tough, armoured skin to protect it from rocks in fast-flowing rivers. It has a short snout and high, smooth skull. Its short snout does not prevent it from eating a lot of fish.

Did you know? Male alligators keep growing until they are 15 years of age.

► MONSTER CROC

The huge Nile crocodile is the biggest and strongest freshwater predator in Africa. It can grow up to 6m long and eats any prey it can overpower, including monkeys, antelopes, zebras and people. Nile crocodiles probably kill at least 300 people a year in Africa. Despite its name, the Nile crocodile is not just found along the Nile but also lives in rivers, lakes and swamps through most of tropical Africa.

A Scaly Skin

The outside of a crocodilian's body is completely covered in a suit of leathery armour. It is made up of rows of tough scales, called scutes, that are set into a thick layer of skin. Some scutes have small bony discs inside them. Most crocodilians have bony scutes only on their backs, but some, such as caimans, have them on their bellies as well. The tail never contains bony scutes, but it does have thicker tail scutes. As crocodilians grow, bigger scutes develop under the old ones. Crocodilians do not get rid of their old scaly skin in a big piece, like a snake, or in patches like a lizard. Old scutes drop off one at a time, just as humans lose flakes of skin all the time. On the head, the skin is fused directly to the bones of the skull without any muscles or fat in between.

Tricky Alligator
A Guyanese myth tells how the Sun was tricked by an alligator into letting him guard his fishponds from a thief. The thief was the alligator and to punish him the Sun slashed his body, forming the scales. The alligator promised the Sun his daughter for a wife. He had no children, so he carved her from a tree. The Sun and the woman's offspring were the Carob people.

▲ **COLOUR CHANGE**
Most crocodilians are brightly coloured or patterned as babies, but these features usually fade as they grow older. They have more or less disappeared in the fully-grown adult. The colours and patterns may help with camouflage by breaking up the outline of the body.

▲ **NECK ARMOUR**
Heavy, bony scutes pack tightly together to create a rigid and formidable armour on the back and neck of an African dwarf crocodile. Even the scutes on the sides of its body and tail are heavily armoured. This species lives in the dwindling rainforests of West and Central Africa. The small size and bony armour of the dwarf crocodile has saved it so far from being hunted for its skin.

▲ MISSING SCALES

The gharial has fewer rows of armoured scutes along its back than other crocodilians. Adults have four rows of deeply ridged back scutes, whereas other crocodilians have two or four extra rows in the middle of the back. The scutes on the sides and belly are unarmoured.

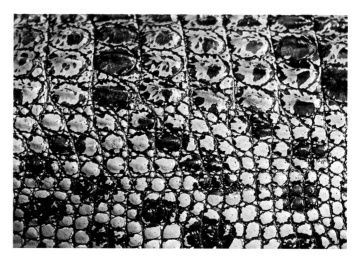

▲ BONY BACK

The belly of a saltwater crocodile does not have bony plates in the scutes. You can see the difference in this close-up. Large, bony back scutes are shown at the top of the picture and the smaller, smoother belly scutes are at the bottom. The scutes are arranged in rows.

► EXTRA ARMOUR

This close-up shows the skin of a dwarf caiman – the most heavily armoured crocodilian. It has strong bones in the scutes on its belly as well as its back. This provides protection from predators. Even its eyelids are protected by bony plates.

Did you know? The scales of the black caiman are as tough as the heel of a boot.

► ALBINO ALLIGATOR

An albino (white) crocodilian would not survive long in the wild. Its colours do not blend in well with its surroundings, making it easy prey. Those born in captivity in zoos or crocodile farms may survive to adulthood. True albinos are white with pink eyes. White crocodilians with blue eyes are not true albinos.

American alligator (*Alligator mississippiensis*)

137

Bodies and Bones

The crocodilian body has changed very little over the last 200 million years. It is superbly adapted to life in the water. Crocodilians can breathe with just their nostrils above the surface. Underwater, ears and nostrils close and a transparent third eyelid sweeps across the eye for protection. Crocodilians are the only reptiles with ear flaps. Inside the long, lizard-like body a bony skeleton supports and protects the lungs, heart, stomach and other soft organs. The stomach is in two parts, one part for grinding food, the other for absorbing (taking in) nutrients. Unlike other reptiles, which have a single-chambered heart, a crocodilian's heart has four chambers, like a mammal. This allows the heart to pump more oxygen-rich blood to the brain during a dive. The thinking part of its brain is more developed than in other reptiles. This enables a crocodilian to learn things rather than act only on instinct.

▲ **THROAT FLAP**
A crocodilian has no lips so it is unable to seal its mouth underwater. Instead, two special flaps at the back of the throat stop water filling the mouth and flowing into the lungs. This enables the crocodile to open its mouth underwater to catch and eat prey without drowning.

Did you know? A saltwater crocodile can stay underwater for more than an hour.

◄ **PREHISTORIC LOOKS**
These American alligators look much like their crocodilian ancestors that lived with the dinosaurs long ago. Crocodilians are the largest living reptiles. The heaviest is the saltwater crocodile which can reach up to 1,100kg.

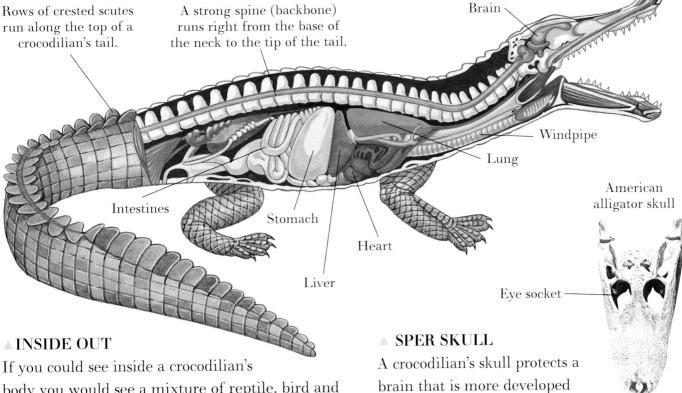

Rows of crested scutes run along the top of a crocodilian's tail.

A strong spine (backbone) runs right from the base of the neck to the tip of the tail.

Brain

Windpipe

Lung

Intestines

Stomach

Heart

Liver

American alligator skull

Eye socket

American crocodile skull

▲ INSIDE OUT

If you could see inside a crocodilian's body you would see a mixture of reptile, bird and mammal features. The crocodilian's brain and shoulder blades are like a bird's. Its heart, diaphragm and efficient breathing system are similar to those of mammals. The stomach and digestive system are those of a reptile, as they deal with food that cannot be chewed.

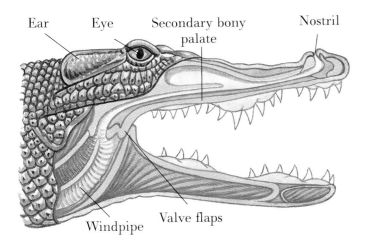

Ear   Eye   Secondary bony palate   Nostril

Windpipe

Valve flaps

▲ WELL DESIGNED

A view inside the head of a crocodilian shows the ear, eye and nostril openings set high up in the skull. The bones in the mouth are joined together to create a secondary bony palate that separates the nostrils from the mouth. Flaps of skin form a valve, sealing off the windpipe underwater.

▲ SPER SKULL

A crocodilian's skull protects a brain that is more developed than any other reptile's. The skull is wider and more rounded in alligators (*top*), and long and triangular in crocodiles (*bottom*). Behind the eye sockets are two large holes where jaw muscles attach to the skull.

▲ STOMACH STONES

Crocodilians swallow objects, such as pebbles, to help break down their food. These gastroliths (stomach stones) churn around inside part of the stomach, helping to cut up food so it can be digested. Some very unusual gastroliths have been found, such as bottles, coins, a whistle and a thermos flask.

139

Jaws and Teeth

The mighty jaws of a crocodilian and its impressive rows of spiky teeth are lethal weapons for catching prey. Crocodilians have two or three times as many teeth as a human. The sharp, jagged teeth at the front of the mouth, called canines, are used to pierce and grip prey. The force of the jaws closing drives these teeth, like a row of knives, deep into a victim's flesh. The short, blunt molar teeth at the back of the mouth are used for crushing prey. Crocodilian teeth are no good for chewing food, and the jaws cannot be moved sideways to chew either. Food has to be swallowed whole, or torn into chunks. The teeth are constantly growing. If a tooth falls out, a new one grows through to replace it.

▲ MEGA JAWS

The jaws of a Nile crocodile close with tremendous force. They sink into their prey with tons of crushing pressure. Yet the muscles that open the jaws are weak. A thick elastic band over the snout can easily hold a crocodile's jaws shut.

◄ NEW TEETH FOR OLD

Each tooth is set in a socket and held in place by connective tissue. Throughout a crocodilian's life, the old teeth fall out and new teeth underneath take their place. Teeth last up to two years before falling out. Alternate teeth are replaced together, so that not all the teeth in one part of the mouth are lost at the same time.

◄ LOTS OF TEETH

The gharial has more teeth than any other crocodilian, around 110. Its teeth are also smaller than those of other crocodilians and are all the same size. The narrow, beak-like snout and long, thin teeth of the gharial are geared to grabbing fish with a sweeping sideways movement of the head. The sharp teeth interlock to trap and impale the slippery prey.

CHARMING

Crocodilian teeth are sometimes made into necklaces. People wear them as decoration or lucky charms. In South America, the Montana people of Peru believe they will be protected from poisoning by wearing a crocodile tooth.

▲ BABY TEETH

A baby American alligator is born with a full set of 80 teeth when it hatches from its egg. Baby teeth are not as sharp as adult teeth and are more fragile. They are like tiny needles. In young crocodiles, the teeth at the back of the mouth usually fall out first. In adults, it is the teeth at the front that are replaced more often.

Did you know? A Nile crocodile may use 45 sets of teeth by the time it is 4m long.

► GRABBING TEETH

A Nile crocodile grasps a lump of prey ready for swallowing. If prey is too large to swallow whole, the crocodile grips the food firmly in its teeth and shakes its head hard so that any unwanted pieces are shaken off.

A Nile crocodile has 68 teeth lining its huge jaws.

On the Move

Have you ever seen a film of an alligator gliding through the water with slow, S-shaped sweeps of its powerful tail? Crocodilians move gracefully and easily in the water, using very little energy and keeping most of their body hidden under the surface. Legs lie close alongside bodies to make them streamlined, and cut down drag from the water. They may be used as rudders to change course. On land, the short legs of crocodilians make their walk look slow and clumsy, but they can move quite fast if they need to. Some can gallop at 18km/h when running for short distances of up to 90m. Crocodilians also move by means of the belly slide. With side-to-side twists of the body the animal uses its legs to push along on its belly. This tobogganing movement is useful for fast escapes, but is also used to slip quietly into the water.

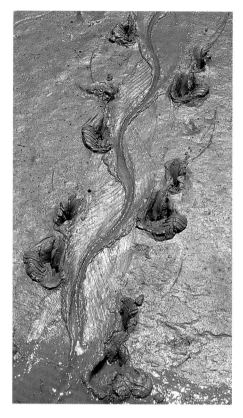

▲ BEST FOOT FORWARD
The tracks of a saltwater crocodile in the mud show how its legs move in sequence. The right front leg goes forwards first, then the back left leg. The front left leg goes forward next and finally the right back leg. If the legs on the same side moved one after the other, the crocodile would overbalance.

▼ THE HIGH WALK
To move overland, crocodilians hold their legs underneath the body, lifting most of the tail off the ground. This is called the high walk. It is very different from the walk of a lizard, which keeps its legs sprawled out at the sides of its body. The tail is dragged behind the body in the high walk, but if the animal starts to run, the tail swings from side to side.
A special ankle joint lets crocodilians twist and turn their legs in the stately high walk.

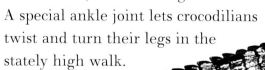

▲ FLOATING AROUND

This Nile crocodile is floating near the surface of Lake Tanganyika, Tanzania, Africa. It is holding its feet out to the sides for balance. The toes and the webbing between them are spread out for extra stability. In the water, the crocodile floats with its tail down, but as it moves its body becomes horizontal.

► TAIL WALKING

Some crocodilians leap straight up out of the water. They seem to be walking on their tails in the same way that a dolphin can travel backwards on its strong tail. This movement is unusual. Large crocodiles will also spring upwards, propelled by the back legs, to grab prey unawares.

► FEET AND TOES

On the front feet, crocodilians have five separate digits (toes). These sometimes have webbing (skin) stretched between them. The back feet are always webbed to help them balance and move in the water. There are only four toes on the back feet. The fifth toe is just a small bone inside the foot.

▲ THE GALLOP

The fastest way for a crocodilian to move on land is to gallop. Only a few crocodiles, such as the Johnston's crocodile shown above, make a habit of moving like this. In a gallop, the back legs push the crocodilian forward in a leap and the front legs stretch out to catch the body as it lands at the end of the leap. Then the back legs swing forward to push the animal forwards again.

Temperature Check

Soon after the sun rises, the first alligators heave themselves out of the river and flop down on the bank. The banks fill up quickly as more alligators join the first, warming their scaly bodies in the sun's rays. As the hours go by and the day becomes hotter, the alligators open their toothy jaws wide to cool down. Later in the day, they may go for a swim or crawl into the shade to cool off. As the air chills at night, the alligators slip back into the water again. This is because water stays warmer for longer at night than the land.

Crocodilians are cold-blooded, which means their body temperature varies with outside temperatures. To warm up or cool down, they move to warm or cool places. Their ideal body temperature is between 30 and 35°C.

▲ **MUD PACK**
A spectacled caiman is buried deep in the mud to keep cool during the hot, dry season. Mud is like water and does not get as hot or as cold as dry land. It also helps to keep the caiman's scaly skin free from parasites and biting insects.

◄ **SOLAR PANELS**
The crested scutes on the tail of a crocodilian are like the bony plates on armoured dinosaurs. They act like solar panels, picking up heat when the animal basks in the sun. The scutes also move apart fractionally to let as much heat as possible escape from the body to cool it down.

◄ UNDER THE ICE

An alligator can survive under a layer of ice as long as it keeps a breathing hole open. Only alligators stay active at temperatures as low as 12 or 15°C. They do not eat, however, because the temperature is too low for their digestions to work.

▼ OPEN WIDE

While a Nile crocodile suns itself on a rock it also opens its mouth in a wide gape. Gaping helps to prevent the crocodile becoming too hot. The breeze flowing over the wide, wet surfaces of the mouth and tongue dries its moisture and, in turn, cools off its blood. If you lick your finger and blow on it softly, you will notice that it feels a lot cooler.

▲ ALLIGATOR DAYS

Alligators follow a distinct daily routine when the weather is good, moving in and out of the water at regular intervals. They also enter the water if they are disturbed. In winter, alligators retreat into dens and become rather sleepy because their blood cools and slows them down.

► MEAL BREAKS

Being cold blooded is quite useful in some ways. These alligators can bask in the sun without having to eat very much or very often. Warm-blooded animals such as mammals have to eat regularly. They need to eat about five times as much food as reptiles to keep their bodies warm.

Crocodilian Senses

The senses of sight, hearing, smell, taste and touch are much more powerful in a crocodilian than in other living reptiles. They have good eyesight and can see in colour. Their eyes are also adapted to seeing well in the dark, which is useful because they hunt mainly at night. Crocodilians also have sharp hearing. They sense the sounds of danger or prey moving nearby and listen for the barks, coughs and roars of their own species at mating time. Crocodilians also have sensitive scales along the sides of their jaws, which help to feel and capture prey.

▲ **NOISY GATORS**

An American alligator bellows loudly during courtship. Noises such as hissing or snarling are made at enemies. Young alligators call for help from adults. Small ear slits behind the eyes are kept open when the animal is out of the water. Flaps close to protect the ears when the animal submerges.

Did you know? Crocodiles shake their ear flaps up and down when they are angry.

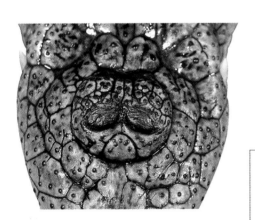

▲ **SMELL DETECTORS**

A Nile crocodile picks up chemical signals through the nostrils at the tip of its snout. These smelly messages help it to detect prey and others of its kind. Crocodiles can smell food over long distances. They are known to have come from as far away as 3km to feed together on the carcass of a large animal.

Crocodile Tears

According to legend, crocodiles cry to make people feel so sorry for them that they come near enough for the crocodiles to catch them. Crocodiles are also supposed to shed tears of remorse before finishing their meal. It is said that people cry crocodile tears when they seem to be sorry for something, but really are not. Real-life crocodiles cannot cry but sometimes look as if they are.

► TASTY TONGUE

Inside the gaping mouth of an American crocodile is a wide, fleshy tongue. It is joined to the bottom of the mouth and does not move, so it plays no part in catching prey. We know that crocodilians have taste buds lining their mouths because some prefer one type of food to another. They can tell the difference between sweet and sour tastes. They also have salt glands on their tongues that get rid of excess salt. Salt builds up in the body over time if the animal lives in the sea or a very dry environment.

◄ GLOW-IN-THE-DARK EYES

A flashlight shone into a crocodile farm at night makes the dark glow eerily with a thousand living lights. The scientific explanation is that a special layer at the back of the eye reflects light back into the front of the eye. This makes sure that the eye catches as much light as possible. Above water, crocodilians see well and are able to spot prey up to 90m away. Under water, an inner, transparent lid covers the eye. This makes their eyesight foggy, rather like looking through thick goggles.

► A PREDATOR'S EYE

The eye of a spectacled caiman, like all crocodilians, has both upper and lower lids. A third eyelid at the side, called a nictating (blinking) membrane, moves across to clean the eye's surface. The dark, vertical pupil narrows to a slit to stop bright light damaging the eye. At night, the pupil opens wide to let any available light into the eye. A round pupil, such as a human's, cannot open as wide.

Food and Hunting

How would it feel to wait up to two years for a meal? Amazingly, a big crocodile can probably survive this long between meals. It lives off fat stored in its tail and other parts of its body. Crocodilians eat a lot of fish, but their strong jaws will snap up anything that wanders too close, from birds, snakes and turtles to raccoons, zebras, cattle and horses. They also eat dead animals. Young crocodilians eat small animals such as insects, snails and frogs.

Most crocodilians sit and wait for their food to come to them, which saves energy. They also catch their meals by stealthily stalking and surprising prey. The three main ways of capturing and killing food are lunging towards prey, leaping up out of the water and sweeping open jaws from side to side through the water. Most crocodilians hunt at night. They eat every part of their prey, including the bones.

▲ **SURPRISE ATTACK**
A Nile crocodile lunges from the water at an incredible speed to grab a wildebeest in its powerful jaws. It is difficult for the wildebeest to jump back as the river bank slopes steeply into the water. The crocodile will plunge back into the water, dragging its prey with it in order to drown it.

▼ **CHEEKY BIRDS**
Large crocodiles feed on big wading birds such as this saddlebill stork. Birds, however, often seem to know when they are in no danger from a crocodile. Plovers have been seen standing on the gums of crocodiles and even pecking at the fearsome teeth for leftovers. A marabou stork was once seen stealing a fish right out of a crocodile's mouth.

▶ SMALLER PREY

A dwarf caiman lies in wait to snap up a tasty bullfrog. Small species of crocodilian like this caiman, as well as young crocodilians, eat a lot of frogs and toads. Youngsters also snap up beetles, spiders, giant water bugs and small fishes. They will leap into the air to catch dragonflies and other insects hovering over the water. Small crocodilians are also preyed upon by their larger relatives.

Crocodilians have varied diets and will eat any animal they can catch.

◀ SWALLOWING PREY

A crocodile raises its head and grips a crab firmly at the back of its throat. After several jerky head movements the crab is correctly positioned to be eaten whole. High levels of acid in the crocodile's stomach help it break down the crab's hard shell so that every part is digested.

Did you know? A Nile crocodile has a stomach that is about the size of a basketball.

▶ FISHY FOOD

A Nile crocodile swallows a fish head first. This stops any spines it has sticking in the crocodile's throat. About 70 per cent of the diet of most crocodilians is fish. Crocodilians with narrow snouts, such as the gharial, Johnston's crocodile and the African slender-snouted crocodile, feed mainly on fish. Fish are caught with a sideways, snapping movement that is easier and faster with a slender snout.

Focus on a

1 A Nile crocodile is nearly invisible as it lies almost submerged in wait for its prey. Only its eyes, ears and nostrils are showing. It lurks in places where it knows prey regularly visit the river. Its dark olive colour provides effective camouflage. To disappear completely it can vanish beneath the water. Some crocodilians can hold their breath for more than an hour while submerged.

A crocodile quietly drifting near the shore looks just like a harmless, floating log. This is just a disguise as it waits for an unsuspecting animal to come down to the river to drink. The crocodile is in luck. A herd of zebras come to cross the river. The crocodile launches its attack with astonishing speed. Shooting forwards it snaps shut its powerful jaws and sharp teeth like a vice around a zebra's leg or muzzle. The stunned zebra is pulled into deeper water to be drowned. Other crocodiles are attracted to the large kill. They gather round to bite into the carcass, rotating in the water to twist off large chunks of flesh. Grazing animals constantly risk death-by-crocodile to drink or cross water. There is little they can do to defend themselves from the attack of such a large predator.

2 The crocodile erupts from the water, taking the zebras by surprise. It lunges at its victim with a quick burst of energy. It is important for the crocodile to overcome its prey quickly as it cannot chase it overland. The crocodile is also easily exhausted and takes a long time to recover from exercise of any kind.

Crocodile's Lunch

3 The crocodile seizes, pulls and shakes the zebra in its powerful jaws. Sometimes the victim's neck is broken in the attack and it dies quickly. More often the shocked animal is dragged into the water, struggling feebly against its attacker.

4 The crocodile drags the zebra into deeper water and holds it down to drown it. It may also spin round in a roll, until the prey stops breathing. The crocodile twists or rolls around over and over again, with the animal clamped in its jaws, until the prey is dead.

5 A freshly killed zebra attracts Nile crocodiles from all around. A large kill is too difficult for one crocodile to defend on its own. Several crocodiles take it in turns to share the feast and may help each other to tear the carcass apart. They fasten their jaws on to a leg or lump of muscle and twist in the water like a rotating shaft, until a chunk of meat is torn loose and can be swallowed.

Communication

Crocodilians pass on messages to each other by means of sounds, body language, smells and touch. Unlike other reptiles, they have a remarkable social life. Groups gather together for basking, sharing food, courting and nesting. Communication begins in the egg and continues throughout life. Adults are particularly sensitive to hatchling and juvenile distress calls and respond with threats or actual attacks. Sounds are made with the vocal cords and with other parts of the body, such as slapping the head against the surface of the water. Crocodilians also use visual communication. Body postures and special movements show which individuals are strong and dominant. Weaker individuals signal to show that they recognize a dominant individual and in this way avoid fighting and injury.

▲ **HEAD BANGER**
A crocodile lifts its head out of the water, jaws open. The jaws slam shut just before they smack the surface of the water. This is called the head slap and makes a loud pop followed by a splash. Head slapping may be a sign of dominance and is often used during the breeding season.

The Fox and the Crocodile
In this Aesop's fable, the fox and the crocodile met one day. The crocodile boasted at length about its cunning as a hunter. Then the fox said, "That's all very impressive, but tell me, what am I wearing on my feet?" The crocodile looked down and there, on the fox's feet, was a pair of shoes made from crocodile skin.

▲ **GHARIAL MESSAGES**
The gharial does not head slap, but claps its jaws under water during the breeding season. Sound travels faster through water than air, so sound signals are very useful for aquatic life.

▶ INFRASOUNDS

Some crocodilians make sounds by rapidly squeezing their torso muscles just beneath the surface of the water. The water bubbles up and bounces off the back. The sounds produced are at a very low level so we can hardly hear them. At close range, they sound like distant thunder. These infrasounds travel quickly over long distances through the water and may be part of courtship. Sometimes they are produced before bellowing, roaring or head slaps.

Did you know? The bellow of an alligator can be heard at least 150m away.

◀ I AM THE GREATEST

Dominant animals are usually bigger and more aggressive than submissive ones. They show off their importance by swimming boldly at the surface or thrashing their tails from side to side on land. Weaker individuals usually only lift their heads out of the water and expose their vulnerable throats. This shows that they submit and do not want to fight.

▶ GETTING TOGETHER

These caimans are gathering together at the start of the rainy season in Brazil. Crocodilians often come together in loose groups, for example when basking, nesting or sharing food. They tend to ignore each other once dominance battles have been established. During a long, dry spell, large numbers of crocodilians often gather together at water holes to share the remaining water. Young crocodilians stay in a close group for the first months of life as there is safety in numbers.

Choosing a Mate

Male and female crocodilians are often difficult to tell apart. Only male gharials are immediately recognizable, distinguished from females by the knob on the end of their snouts. Most males are larger, and grow and mature more quickly than females. They are ready to mate at about seven years old and females at about nine.

In some species, groups of adults gather together in the breeding season and set up special mating territories. In other species, mating takes place in long-established territories. Females often begin the courtship process. Courtship behaviour includes bellowing and grunting, rubbing heads and bodies, blowing bubbles, circling and riding on the partner's back.

▲ POT NOSE
Most male gharials have a strange bump, or pot, on the end of the snout near the nostrils. Females have flat snouts. No-one is quite sure what the pot is for, but it is probably used in courtship. It may help the male to change hissing sounds into buzzing sounds as air vibrates inside the hollow pot.

◀ COURTING COUPLE
Crocodilians touch each other a lot during courtship, especially around the head and neck. Males will also try to impress females by bubbling water from the nostrils and mouth. An interested female arches her back, then raises her head with her mouth open. The two may push each other under the water to see how big and strong their partner is.

◄ SWEET-SMELLING SCENT

Crocodilians have little bumps under their lower jaws. These are musk glands. The musk is a sweet-smelling, greenish, oily perfume. It produces a scent that attracts the opposite sex. Musk glands are more noticeable in males. During courtship, the male may rub his throat across the female's head and neck. This releases the scent from the musk glands and helps to prepare the female for mating.

► FIGHTING MALES

Male crocodilians may fight each other for the chance to court and mate with females. They may spar with their jaws open or make themselves look bigger and more powerful by puffing up their bodies with air. Saltwater crocodiles are particularly violent and bash their heads together with a loud thud. These contests may go on for an hour or more but do not seem to cause much permanent damage.

◄ THE MATING GAME

Courtship can last for up to two hours before mating occurs. The couple sink under the water and the male wraps his tail around his partner. Mating takes only a few minutes. The couple mate several times during the day. A dominant male may mate with up to 20 females in the breeding season. Females, too, mate with other males, although the dominant male tries to prevent this.

Focus on

Early in April or May, American alligators begin courtship rituals. Males fight each other to win their own territories. The biggest and strongest males win the best territories. Their musk glands give off a strong, sweet smell, attractive to females. Female alligators do not have territories. They visit the territories of several males and may mate several times. Once a female and a male have mated, they part. The female builds a nest in June or July and lays her eggs. In about 60 to 70 days, the young alligators begin to hatch and the female digs them out of the nest and carries them to water. She remains with her young for months or even years.

1 Male and female alligators do not live together all year round. They come together in spring to court and mate. The rest of the year they glide through the swamp, searching for food or basking in the sun. In winter they rest in cosy dens.

2 The American alligator is the noisiest crocodilian. Males and females make bellowing noises especially in the breeding season. Males bellow loudly to warn other males to keep out of their territories and to let females know where they are. Each alligator has a different voice, which sounds like the throaty roar of a stalling motorboat engine. The sound carries for long distances in the swamp. Once one alligator starts to bellow, others soon join in and may carry on for half an hour.

Alligators

3 In the mating season bulls (males) test each other to see which is the biggest and strongest. They push and wrestle and sometimes fight violently. The strongest males win the best territories for food and water. Bellowing helps to limit serious fighting. Other males stay away from areas where they have heard a loud bull.

4 Alligators mate in shallow water. Before mating, there is a slow courtship made up of slapping the water and rubbing each other's muzzle and neck. Mating usually lasts only a minute or two before the pair separate. Alligators may mate with several partners in a season.

5 The female alligator uses her body, legs and tail to build a nest out of sand, soil and plants. It takes about two weeks to build and may be up to 75cm high and 2m across. In the middle the female digs a hole and lines it with mud. She lays between 20 and 70 eggs, which she then covers up. She stays near the nest site while the eggs develop, guarding them from raccoons and other predators.

Building a Nest

About a month after mating, a female crocodilian is ready to lay her eggs on land. First she builds a nest to keep her eggs warm. If the temperature stays below 28°C, the babies will die before they hatch. The temperature inside the nest determines whether the hatchlings are male or female. Females build their nests at night. Alligators, caimans and some crocodiles build nests that are solid mounds of fresh plants and soil. Other crocodiles, and gharials, dig holes in the sand with their back feet. Some species dig trial nests before they dig the real one. This may be to check that the temperature is right for the eggs to develop. Nest sites are chosen to be near water but above the floodwater mark. The females often stay close to the nest to guard it against predators, even while searching for food.

▲ **SHARING NESTS**
Turtles, such as this red-bellied turtle, sometimes lay their eggs in crocodilian nests to save them the hard work of making their own nests. The eggs are protected by the fierce crocodilian mother, who guards her own eggs and the turtle's eggs. As many as 200 red-bellied turtle eggs have been found in alligator nests.

◀ **NEST MOUNDS**
A Morelet's crocodile has scratched soil and uprooted plant material into a big pile to build her nest mound. She uses her body to press it all together firmly. Then she scoops out a hole in the mound with her back feet. She lays her eggs in the hole and then closes the top of the nest. As the plant material rots, it gives off heat, which keeps the eggs warm.

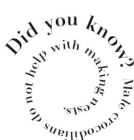
Did you know? Male crocodilians do not help with making nests.

▼ IS IT A BOY OR A GIRL?

A saltwater crocodile, like all crocodilians, keeps its eggs at about 30 to 32°C inside the nest. The temperatures during the first few weeks after the eggs are laid is crucial. This controls whether the babies are male or female. Higher temperatures, such as 32–33°C produce more males, while temperatures of 31°C or lower produce more females. Temperature also affects the colour and body patterns of the babies.

▲ A SANDY NEST

Nile crocodiles dig their nests on sandy river banks, beaches or lakesides. Females may compete for nest sites by trying to push each other over. Larger, heavier females usually win these contests. The female uses her back legs for digging, so the nest burrow is dug to a depth of about the same length as her back legs.

► NESTING TOGETHER

Female Nile crocodiles often nest together. A female may even return to the same breeding ground and nest site each year. Each female guards her nest, either by lying right on top of the nest or watching it from the nearby shade.

◄ NEST THIEF

The monitor lizard often digs its way into crocodile nests in Africa and Asia to eat the eggs. In Africa, these lizards may sometimes steal over half of all the eggs laid.

159

Developing Eggs

All crocodilians lay white, oval eggs with hard shells like those of a bird. The number of eggs laid by one female at a time varies from about 10 to 90, depending on the species and the age of the mother. Older females lay more eggs. The length of time it takes for the eggs to hatch varies with the species and the temperature, but takes from 55 to 110 days. During this time, called the incubation period, the weather can affect the babies developing inside the eggs. Too much rain can drown the babies before they are born as water can seep through the shells. Hot weather may cause the inside of the egg to overheat. This hardens the yolk so that the baby cannot absorb it and starves to death. Another danger is that eggs laid by one female are accidentally dug up and destroyed by another female digging a nest in the same place.

▲ EGGY HANDFUL
In many countries, people eat crocodilian eggs. They harvest them from nests for sale at the local market. This person is holding the eggs of a gharial. Each egg weighs about 100g. The mother gharial lays about 40 eggs in a hole in the sand. She lays them in two tiers, separated from each other by a fairly thick layer of sand, and may spend several hours covering her nest.

▶ LAYING EGGS
The mugger, or swamp, crocodile of India digs a sandy pit about 50cm deep in a river bank and lays 10 to 50 eggs inside. She lays her eggs in layers and then covers them with a mound of twigs, leaves, soil and sand. During the 50-to 75-day incubation, the female spends most of the time practically on top of the nest. When females lay their eggs, they are usually quite tame. Researchers have been able to catch the eggs as they are laid.

▶ INSIDE AN EGG

Curled tightly inside its egg, this alligator has its head and tail twisted around its belly. Next to the developing baby is a supply of yolk, which provides it with food during incubation. Researchers have removed the top third of the shell to study the stages of development. The baby will develop normally even though some of the shell is missing. As the eggs develop, they give off carbon dioxide gas into the nest. This reacts with air in the chamber and may make the shell thinner to let in more oxygen.

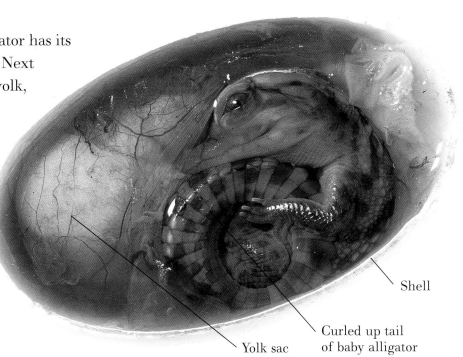

Shell

Curled up tail of baby alligator

Yolk sac

◀ CRACKING EGGS

Mother crocodiles sometimes help eggs to hatch. When she hears the baby calling inside, she picks up the egg in her mouth. Holding it gently, she rolls the egg to and fro against the roof of her mouth, pressing gently to crack the shell. The mother may have to do this for around 20 minutes before the baby breaks free from the egg.

Did you know? A large crocodile may take an hour to lay 80 or more eggs.

▶ EGGS IN THE NEST

Saltwater crocodiles lay large, creamy-white eggs, up to twice the size of chickens' eggs. However, the eggs are more equally rounded at each end than chicken's eggs. It takes a female saltwater crocodile about 15 minutes to lay between 20 and 90 eggs in her nest. The eggs take up to 90 days to hatch.

Focus on

Baby crocodilians make yelping, croaking and grunting noises from inside their eggs when it is time to hatch. The mother hears the noise and digs the eggs from the nest. The babies struggle free of their eggshells, sometimes with help from their mother. While the young are hatching the mother is in a very aggressive mood and will attack any animal that comes near. The hatchlings are about 28cm long, lively and very agile. They can give a human finger a painful nip with their sharp teeth. Their mother carries them gently in her mouth down to the water. She opens her jaws and waggles her head from side to side to wash the babies out of her mouth.

1 As soon as a mother Nile crocodile hears her babies calling from inside their eggs, she knows it is time to help them escape from the nest. She scrapes away the soil and sand with her front feet and may even use her teeth to cut through any roots that have grown between the eggs. Her help is very important as the soil has hardened during incubation. The hatchlings would find it difficult to dig their way up to the surface without her help.

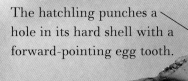

The hatchling punches a hole in its hard shell with a forward-pointing egg tooth.

2 This baby Nile crocodile has just broken through its eggshell. It used a horny tip on the snout, called the egg tooth, to break through. The egg tooth is the size of a grain of sand and disappears after about a week. The egg has become thinner during the long incubation. This makes it easier for the baby to break free.

Hatching Out

3 Struggling out of an egg is a long, exhausting process for the hatchling. When the babies are half out of their eggs, they sometimes take a break so they can rest before completely leaving their shells. After hatching, the mother crushes or swallows rotten eggs.

4 Even though they are fierce predators crocodilians make caring parents. The mother Nile crocodile lowers her head into the nest and delicately picks up the hatchlings, as well as any unhatched eggs, between her sharp teeth. She gulps them into her mouth. The weight of all the babies and eggs pushes down on her tongue to form a pouch that holds up to 20 eggs and live young. Male mugger crocodiles also carry the young like this and help hatchlings to escape from their eggs.

5 A young crocodilian's belly looks fat when it hatches. This is because it contains the remains of the yolk sac, which nourished it through the incubation period. The hatchling can swim and catch its own food straight away, but it continues to feed on the yolk sac for up to two weeks. In Africa, the wet season usually starts soon after baby Nile crocodiles hatch. This provides an abundance of food, such as insects, tadpoles and frogs for the hatchlings. They are very vulnerable to predators and are guarded by their mother for at least the first weeks of life.

Growing Up

Juvenile (young) crocodilians lead a very dangerous life. They are too small to defend themselves easily, despite their sharp teeth. Their bright colours also make them easy for predators to spot. All sorts of predators lurk in the water and on the shore, from birds of prey and monitor lizards to otters, pelicans, tiger fish and even other crocodilians. One of the reasons that crocodilians lay so many eggs is that so many young do not survive to reach their first birthday. Only one in ten alligators lives to the end of its first year. Juveniles often stay together in groups during the first weeks of life and call loudly to the adults for help if they are in danger. By the time the juveniles are four years old, they stop making distress calls and start responding to the calls of other young individuals.

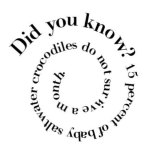

▲ INSECT DIET

A spiky-jawed Johnston's crocodile is about to snap up a damselfly. Juveniles eat mainly insects. As they grow, they take larger prey, such as snails, shrimps, crabs and small fish. Their snouts gradually strengthen, so that they are able to catch bigger prey. At a few months old, they live rather like lizards and move quite a distance away from the water.

Did you know? 15 percent of baby saltwater crocodiles do not survive a month

◄ FAST FOOD

These juvenile alligators will grow twice as fast in captivity as they would in the wild. This is because they are fed regular meals and do not have to wait until they can catch a meal for themselves. It is also because they are kept in warm water – alligators stop feeding in cooler water. The best temperature for growth is 30–32°C.

▶ BABY CARRIERS

Juveniles stay close to their mother for the first few weeks, often using her back to rest on. No predator would dare to attack them there. Baby alligators are only about 25cm long when they are born but they grow very quickly. When they have enough food to eat, male alligators grow about 30cm a year until they are 15 years of age.

▲ CROC CRECHE

A Nile crocodile guards her young while they bask in the sun. A group of crocodilian young is called a pod. A pod may stay in the same area for as long as two years. At the first sign of danger, the mother rapidly vibrates her trunk muscles and the young immediately dive underwater.

▲ TOO MANY ENEMIES

The list of land predators that attack juvenile crocodilians include big cats such as this leopard, ground hornbills, marabou storks and genet cats. Large wading birds, including herons, spear them with their sharp beaks in shallow water, while, in deeper water, catfish, otters and turtles all enjoy a young crocodilian as a snack. Only about two per cent of all the eggs laid each year survive to hatch and grow into adults.

▶ NOISY POD

A pod of juveniles, like this group of young caimans, is a noisy bunch. By chirping and yelping for help, a juvenile warns its brothers and sisters that there is a predator nearby. The siblings quickly dive for shelter and hope that an adult will come to protect them. If a young Nile crocodile strays from its pod, it makes loud distress calls. Its mother, or any other female nearby, will pick up the youngster in her jaws and carry it back to the group.

On the Defensive

By the time a crocodilian has grown to about 1m long, very few predators will threaten it. The main dangers to adult crocodilians come from large animals, such as jaguars, lions, elephants, and hippopotamuses, who attack to protect their young. Giant snakes called anacondas will attack and kill crocodilians for food. Adults may also be killed during battles with other crocodilians during the breeding season. People are the Number One enemy of crocodilians. They kill them for their skins, for food or because they are dangerous. Crocodilians are protected by their powerful jaws, strong tail and heavy armour. They can also swim away from danger and hide under the water, in the mud or among plants.

▲ KEEP AWAY!
An American alligator puffs up its body with air to look bigger and more threatening. It lets out the air quickly to make a hissing sound. If an enemy is still not scared away, the alligator will then attack.

▶ THE HIDDEN EYE
What sort of animal is peeping out from underneath a green carpet of floating water plants? It is hard to tell that there is a saltwater crocodile lurking just beneath the surface. Crocodilians feel safer in the water because they are such good swimmers. They may spend hours almost completely under water, keeping very still, waiting for prey to come by or for danger to pass. They move so quietly and smoothly that the vegetation on top of the water is hardly disturbed.

▶ CAMOUFLAGE COLOURS

The colour of crocodilians blends in well with their surroundings. Many species change colour all the time. For example, at warmer times of the day, they may become lighter in colour. In cool parts of the day, such as the morning, they may look duller and are often mistaken for logs.

◀ CAIMAN FOR LUNCH

A deadly anaconda squeezes the life out of an unfortunate caiman. The anaconda of South America lives partly in the water and can grow up to 9m long. It can easily kill a caiman by twisting its strong coils around the caiman's body until the victim cannot breathe any more. The caiman dies slowly, either from suffocation or shock. However, anacondas only kill caimans occasionally – they are not an important part of the snake's diet.

Ticking Croc
One of the most famous crocodiles in literature is in Peter Pan, *written by J. M. Barrie in 1904. Peter Pan's greatest enemy is Captain Hook. In a fair fight, Peter cut off Hook's left hand, which is eaten by a crocodile. The crocodile follows Hook's ship, hoping for a chance to gobble up the rest of him. It makes a ticking noise as it travels because it swallowed a clock. At the end, Hook falls into the water. He is chased by the crocodile, but we do not find out if he eats him.*

▲ HUMAN DANGERS

People have always killed small numbers of crocodilians for food, as this Brazilian family have done. However, the shooting of crocodilians through fear or for sport has had a far more severe impact on their population. Of the 22 species of crocodilian, 17 have been hunted to the verge of extinction.

Freshwater Habitats

A habitat is a place where an animal lives. Most crocodilians live in freshwater (not salty) habitats, such as rivers, lakes, marshes and swamps, in warm places. They tend to live in the shallow areas on the edge of the water because they need to be able to crawl on to dry land for basking and laying their eggs. The shallow water also has many plants to hide among and plenty of animals to eat. The temperature of the water does not vary as much as temperatures on dry land do. This helps a crocodilian keep its body temperature steady. Crocodilians save energy by moving about in water rather than on dry land, because the water supports their heavy bodies. Crocodilians also make an impact on their habitats. The American alligator, for example, digs holes in the river bed. These are cool places where alligators and other animals hide during the heat of the day.

▲ **GATOR HOLES**
American alligators living in the Florida Everglades dig large gator holes in the limestone river bed. In the dry season, these holes stay full of water. They provide a vital water supply that keeps the alligators and many other animals alive.

▲ **RIVER DWELLERS**
The gharial likes fast-flowing rivers with high banks, clear water and deep pools where there are plenty of fish. It inhabits rivers such as the Indus in Pakistan, the Ganges in India and the Brahmaputra of Bangladesh and Assam.

Aboriginal Creation Myth
Crocodiles are often shown in bark paintings and rock art made by the Aboriginals of Australia. Their creation myth, called the dream time, tells how ancestral animals created the land and people. According to a Gunwinggu  *story from Arnhem Land, the Liverpool River was made by a crocodile ancestor. The mighty crocodile made his way from the mountains to the sea, chewing the land as he went. This made deep furrows, which filled with water to become the river.*

◄ SEASONAL CHANGE

During the dry season, caimans gather in the few remaining pools along a drying-up river bed. Although the pools become very crowded, the caimans seem to get along well together. In some parts of South America, caimans are forced to live in river pools for four or five months of the year. After the floods of the wet season, they can spread out again.

► NILE CROCODILES

Nile crocodiles warm themselves in the sun on a sandy riverbank. Despite their name, Nile crocodiles do not live only in the river Nile. At one time, these powerful crocodiles lived all over Africa, except in the desert areas. Nowadays, they still live in parts of the Nile, as well as the other African waterways such as the Limpopo and Senegal rivers, Lake Chad and the Okavango swamp. There are also Nile crocodiles living on the island of Madagascar.

◄ AUSTRALIAN HABITATS

Australian crocodiles, such as Johnston's crocodile, often live in billabongs (waterholes) such as this one in the Northern Territory of Australia. They provide crocodiles with water and land as well as food to eat. A billabong is a branch of a river that comes to a dead end. Saltwater crocodiles are also found in such areas because they live in both fresh and salt water. People are advised not to swim or wade in the water and to avoid camping nearby.

Rainforest Dwellers

Three unusual crocodilians live in rainforest streams and swamps where they avoid competition with larger caimans and crocodiles. Cuvier's dwarf caiman and Schneider's dwarf caiman live in South America, while the African dwarf crocodile lives in the tropical forests of Central Africa. The bodies of these small crocodilians are heavily armoured. This may help to protect the South American caimans from sharp rocks in the fast-flowing streams where they live and from spiky plants in the forest. All three crocodilians may also need this extra protection from predators because of their small size. Rainforest crocodilians do not usually bask in the sun during the day, although the dwarf crocodile may sometimes climb trees to sun itself. All three crocodilians seem to spend quite a lot of time on land. Schneider's dwarf caiman lives in burrows dug in stream banks.

▲ **MYSTERY CROC**

Very little is known about the African dwarf crocodile. It is a secretive and shy animal that is active at night. It lives in swamps, ponds and small, slow-moving streams. After heavy rain, the dwarf crocodile may make long trips over land at night. Females lay about ten eggs, which take 100 days to hatch. They probably protect their young in their first weeks.

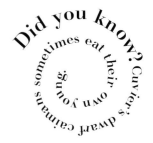

Did you know? Cuvier's dwarf caimans sometimes eat their own young.

◀ **YOUNG COLOURS**

A newly hatched Cuvier's dwarf caiman rests on a rock. Hatchling dwarf caimans have a yellowish-brown skull and black or brown cross bands on the body and tail. This gives good camouflage. For the first couple of days, they are also covered in slime. Then they enter the water for the first time.

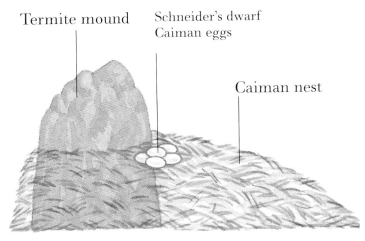

Termite mound

Schneider's dwarf
Caiman eggs

Caiman nest

Termite
mound

Edge of nest

28°C
28.5°C
29°C
30°C
32°C
34°C

1 metre

◄ HELPFUL NEIGHBOURS

Schneider's dwarf caiman lays its eggs beside termite mounds. Little sun reaches the forest floor, so the extra heat generated by the termites helps the caiman's eggs develop. Often, the termites cover the eggs with a rock-hard layer, so the parents must help their young break out.

▲ NOSE TO TAIL

Unlike other caimans, dwarf caimans do not have bony ridges around the eyes and snout. Because of this they are also known as smooth-fronted caimans. Shown here is Cuvier's dwarf caiman. Its short snout is not streamlined for swimming and it has a short tail, which may help it to move more easily on land.

◄ TEETH AND DIET

The sharp, pointed teeth of Cuvier's dwarf caiman curve backwards in the mouth. This helps it grip the slippery skin of frogs or seize such prey as fish in fast-flowing waters. The Cuvier's diet is not well known, but it probably eats a variety of aquatic invertebrates (animals without a backbone), such as shrimps and crabs, as well as rodents, birds and snakes.

MARKINGS FOR LIFE

A black caiman hatches from its egg. Its mother laid up to 65 eggs in the nest, which hatched six weeks later. Its strong markings stay as it grows.

THE SPECTACLED CAIMAN

The spectacled caiman is so-called because of the bony ridges around its eye sockets and across the top of the muzzle. These look a bit like eye glasses and may help to strengthen its skull as it seizes and kills prey.

BIG HEAD

The broad-snouted caiman has the widest head of any crocodilian, with a ridge running down the snout. It is about 2m long and lives in marshes or small streams with dense vegetation.

Focus on

Caimans are mostly small, agile crocodilians that live in Central or South America. Most do not grow more than 2.4m long, but the black caiman can be bigger than an alligator (their closest relative). Caimans look like alligators because their lower teeth do not show when their mouths are closed. They have sharper, longer teeth than alligators and strong, bony plates on the belly and back, including eight bony scutes on the back of the neck. This bony armour helps to protect them from predators, even humans (as tough skin is unsuitable for leather goods). Many caimans are endangered, but some spectacled caimans are very adaptable. They have taken over habitats where American crocodiles and black caimans have been hunted to extinction.

Caimans

Young caimans and alligators have spots and bands across the body.

Black caiman
(Melanosuchus niger)

Bony scutes.

Unusual webbed front feet.

Short, low snout with jaws lined with 64 teeth.

TYPICAL CAIMAN

Caimans have short snouts, roughly circular eye sockets and wrinkled eyelids. Although caimans are closely related to alligators, they are quicker and move more like crocodiles.

EGG THIEF

Tegu lizards eat caiman eggs. In some areas, over 80 per cent of the nests are destroyed by these large lizards. Female caimans may nest together to help defend their eggs.

CAPABLE CAIMAN

The black caiman is the largest of all caimans. The one shown here has just snapped up a piranha fish. Black caimans can grow to over 6m long and have keen eyesight and hearing. They hunt for capybaras (South American rodents) and fish after dusk. When black caimans disappear, the balance of life in an area is upset. Hunted for killing cattle, they are now an endangered species.

Saltwater Species

Most crocodilians live in fresh water, but a few venture into estuaries (the mouths of rivers), coastal swamps or the sea. American and Nile crocodiles and spectacled caimans have been found in saltwater habitats. The crocodilian most often seen at sea is the saltwater crocodile, also known as the Indopacific or estuarine crocodile. It is found over a vast area, from southern India to Fiji in the Pacific Ocean, and although usually found in rivers and lakes, it has been seen hundreds of kilometres from the nearest land. "Saltie" hatchlings are even reared in seawater. This species has efficient salt glands on its tongue to get rid of extra salt without losing too much water. It is a mystery why freshwater crocodiles also have these glands, but it may be because their ancestors lived in the sea. Alligators and caimans do not have salt glands.

▲ SALTY TONGUE
Crocodiles have up to 40 salt glands on the tongue. These special salivary glands allow the crocodile to get rid of excess salt without losing too much water. These glands are necessary because crocodiles have kidneys that need plenty of fresh water to flush out the salt. At sea there is too little fresh water for this to happen.

► SCALY DRIFTER
Although it can swim vast distances far out to sea, a saltwater crocodile is generally a lazy creature. Slow, side-to-side sweeps of a long, muscular tail propel the crocodile through the water, using as little energy as possible. Saltwater crocodiles do not like to have to swim vigorously, so they avoid strong waves wherever possible. They prefer to drift with the tide in relatively calm water.

▶ NEW WORLD CROC

The American crocodile is the most widespread crocodile in the Americas, ranging from southern Florida, USA, to the Pacific coat of Peru. It grows up to 6m in length (3.4m on average) and lives in mangrove swamps, estuaries and lagoons as well as fresh and brackish (slightly salty) coastal rivers. It has the least armour (bony scutes) of any crocodilian and a hump on the snout between the eyes and nostrils.

◀ TRAVELLING CAIMANS

A group of baby spectacled, or common, caimans hides among the leaves of aquatic plants. This wide-ranging species lives in all sorts of habitats, including saltwater ones, such as salt marshes. They even live on islands, such as Trinidad and Tobago in the Caribbean.

◀ LOST ARMOUR

A saltwater crocodile has less protective armour on the neck and back compared to other crocodilians. This makes it easier for the crocodile to bend its body when swimming. Thick, heavy scales would weigh it down too much at sea.

▲ NILE CROCODILE

Nile crocodiles typically live in rivers, but they also inhabit salty estuaries and mangrove swamps. Sometimes they are found on Kenyan beaches and may be swept out to sea. Some have reached the islands of Zanzibar and Madagascar.

175

Ancient Crocodiles

The first alligators and crocodiles lived at the same time as the dinosaurs. Some were even powerful enough to kill the biggest plant-eating dinosaurs. Unlike the dinosaurs, the crocodilians have managed to survive to the present day, possibly because they were so well adapted to their environment. The first crocodiles, the protosuchians, lived about 200 million years ago. They were small land animals with long legs and short snouts. From 200 to 65 million years ago, long-snouted mesosuchians lived mainly in the sea, while the dinosaurs dominated the land. The closest ancestors of today's crocodilians were the early eusuchians, which developed about 80 million years ago. They looked rather like gharials, with long snouts, and probably lurked in the shallow fresh water of rivers and swamps. Like today's crocodilians, the eusuchians could breathe through their nostrils even when their mouths were open underwater. This made it possible for them to catch their prey in the water.

▲ FIRST CROCODILE

The name of this ancient crocodile, *Protosuchus*, means first crocodile. It lived about 200 million years ago in Arizona and looked rather like a lizard. *Protosuchus* was small, probably no more than 1m long, with a small, flat skull and a short snout.

▼ BACK TO THE SEA

Swimming along the shores and estuaries in Jurassic times, from about 200 to 145 million years ago, the most widespread crocodilian was *Stenosaurus*. It looked rather like modern-day gharials, although it is not related to them. *Stenosaurus* had a flexible body and a powerful tail, which allowed it to swim after fast-moving prey.

Long, slender snout and up to 200 piercing teeth for trapping fish.

▶ DINOSAUR DAYS

Goniopholis, shown here, was more dependent on land than many of its fellow mesosuchians. It looked rather like a broad-snouted crocodile of today. *Goniopholis* had two or more rows of armour on its back and well-developed armour on its belly as well. Most mesosuchians lived in the sea. They were long-snouted with many piercing teeth for catching fish.

◀ MONSTER CROCODILE

Lurking in the rivers and lakes of 70 million years ago was a gigantic crocodile called *Deinosuchus*, which grew perhaps 15m long. It was a similar size to *T. rex* and big enough to eat quite large dinosaurs, such as the duck-billed dinosaurs. It had strong teeth and legs, vertebrae (spine bones) that were each 30cm long and heavy protective scales shielding the body and the tail.

▶ SURVIVORS

Crocodilians are survivors of a world inhabited by dinosaurs. However, the origins of both dinosaurs and crocodilians date back much further, to a group of animals called thecodontians, which lived some 200 million years ago.

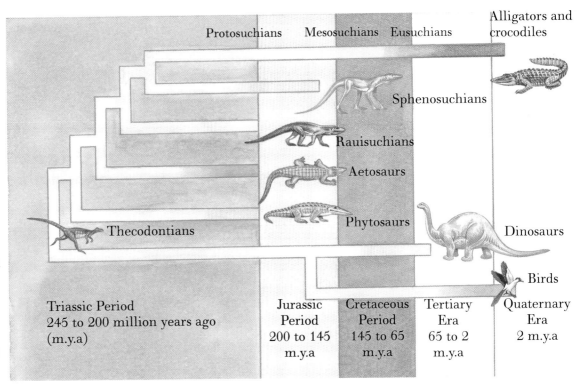

Protosuchians   Mesosuchians   Eusuchians

Alligators and crocodiles

Sphenosuchians

Rauisuchians

Aetosaurs

Thecodontians

Phytosaurs

Dinosaurs

Birds

| Triassic Period 245 to 200 million years ago (m.y.a) | Jurassic Period 200 to 145 m.y.a | Cretaceous Period 145 to 65 m.y.a | Tertiary Era 65 to 2 m.y.a | Quaternary Era 2 m.y.a |

177

Living Relatives

Although it seems strange, birds are probably the closest living relatives of crocodilians. Crocodilians and birds have a long outer ear canal, a muscular gizzard to grind up food and a heart made up of four chambers. They both build nests and look after their young. The next closest living relatives of crocodilians are the group of reptiles called lepidosaurs, which includes the tuatara of New Zealand, lizards and snakes. The skin of lepidosaurs is usually covered by overlapping scales made of keratin (the substance fingernails are made of). Crocodilians and lepidosaurs both have two large openings on the cheek region of the skull, called a diapsid skull. Crocodilians are also more distantly related to the other main group of reptiles, turtles and tortoises.

▼ **DINOSAUR SURVIVOR**

The rare tuatara is found only on a few islands off the north coast of New Zealand. Here there are no rats or dogs to eat their eggs and hatchlings. They have hardly changed in appearance for millions of years and first appeared before dinosaurs lived on Earth.

▲ **NESTING HABITS**

The nests of some birds, such as this mallee fowl, are very similar to those of crocodilians. The mallee fowl builds a huge mound of wet leaves and twigs covered with wet sand. The female then lays her eggs in the middle of the mound.

▲ **A SANDY NEST**

Green turtles live in the sea, but lay their eggs on sandy beaches. The female drags herself up the beach and digs a hole in which to lay her eggs. Then she returns to the sea, leaving the baby turtles to fend for themselves when they eventually hatch.

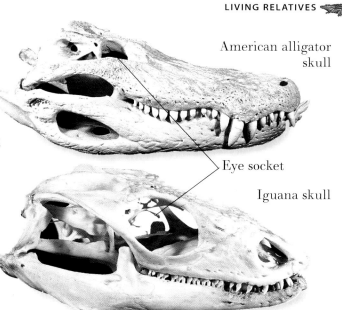

American alligator
skull

Eye socket

Iguana skull

▶ DIAPSID SKULLS

Crocodilians, and lizards such as iguanas, both
have two large openings on each side of the
skull behind the eye sockets. One of these windows
is high on the roof of the skull, the other is down on
the side of the cheek. These openings may be to
make the skull lighter. They also provide areas for
the jaw muscles to join on to the skull, making it
stronger and more powerful. In birds, the two
openings have largely disappeared. Mammals
have only one opening on each side not two, while
turtles have no openings at all.

Red-tailed boa

▲ REPTILE PREDATOR

Snakes are also scaly, meat-eating
reptiles, but they catch prey in very
different ways from a crocodilian.
They have delicate bodies and need to
overpower prey quickly before it can inflict an
injury. Some, such as this boa, squeeze their prey to death in their
powerful coils. Others kill their prey with a poisonous bite.

Did you know? The sex of baby turtles is also controlled by temperature

▶ MONSTROUS
LIZARD

The gila monster of North America is
a lizard with small, bead-like scales. It
is one of the world's two poisonous
lizards and its bright colours are a
warning sign of its poisonous nature.
The poison is produced in glands in
the bottom jaw and chewed into both
predators and prey. Crocodilians have
much larger scales than lizards, and
none are poisonous.

179

Living with People

Many people only ever see a crocodile or an alligator in a story book, on the television or at the cinema. These crocodilians are often huge, fierce monsters that attack and eat humans. Such images have given crocodilians a bad name. A few large crocodiles, such as Nile and saltwater species, can be very dangerous, but most are timid creatures that are no threat to humans. Some people even keep baby crocodilians as pets. Humans are a much bigger threat to crocodilians than they are to us. People hunt them for their skins to make handbags, shoes and belts. Traditional Oriental medicines are made from many of their body parts. Their bones are ground up to add to fertilizers and animal feed. Their meat and eggs are cooked and eaten, while perfume is made from their sex organs, musk and urine.

▲ **ALLIGATOR DANGER**
The just-seen head of an American alligator reinforces why swimming is not allowed. Alligators lurking under the water do occasionally attack people. This usually only happens when humans have invaded its habitat or disturbed its nests or hatchlings.

▶ **CROCODILE DUNDEE**
One of the most dangerous and aggressive crocodilians is the saltwater crocodile, which appeared in the film *Crocodile Dundee*. In the film, Mick "Crocodile" Dundee, saves an American journalist from a surprise attack by a saltie. An adult saltie can grow up to 7m long and is likely to view a human entering its territory as a possible meal.

Krindlekrax

In Philip Ridley's 1991 story, Krindlekrax, *a baby crocodile from a zoo escapes into a sewer and grows enormous on a diet of discarded toast. It becomes the mysterious monster Krindlekrax, which lurks beneath the pavements of Lizard Street. It is eventually tamed by the hero of the book, weedy Ruskin Splinter, who wedges a medal down the crododile's throat. He agrees to take the medal away if Krindlekrax will go back to the sewer and never come back to Lizard Street again.*

▲ SKINS FOR SALE

These saltwater crocodile skins are being processed for tanning. Tanning converts the hard, horny, preserved skin into soft, flexible leather that can be made into bags, wallets, shoes and other goods. Some of the most valuable skins come from saltwater crocodiles, because they have small scales that have few bony plates inside.

▲ ALLIGATOR WALKABOUT

An American alligator walks through a campsite, giving the campers a close-up view. Attacks out of the water are unlikely – the element of surprise is lost and alligators cannot move fast. Meetings like this are harmless.

A false, glass eye has been inserted into the head.

► TOURIST SOUVENIRS

A baby Siamese crocodile was killed so that its head could be made into a key ring as a tourist souvenir. Most tourists never manage to see a wild crocodilian, but if they buy souvenirs such as this, it means more animals will be killed for a cruel trade.

Rare Crocodilians

Almost half of all of crocodilian species are endangered, even though there is much less hunting today than in the past. Until the 1970s, five to ten million crocodilians were being killed each year – far too many for them to reproduce and build up their numbers again. Today, the loss of habitat is a greater threat than hunting for most crocodiles. Other problems include illegal hunting, trapping for food and medicine, and the harvesting of crocodile eggs. Many species are not properly protected in national parks and there are not enough crocodilians being reared on farms and ranches to make sure each species does not disappear for ever. The four most endangered species are the Chinese alligator, the Philippine, Siamese and the Orinoco crocodiles. Other species that only live in small populations are the Cuban crocodile, black caiman and the gharial.

▲ **HABITAT DESTRUCTION**
The trees beside this billabong in Australia have died because there is too much salt in the water. Farmers removed many of the bush plants, which used to trap salt and stop it sinking down into the ground. Now much of the land is ruined by high levels of salt and it is difficult for crocodilians and other wildlife to live there.

► **FISHING COMPETITION**
People fishing for sport as well as for food create competition for crocodilians in some areas. They may also accidentally trap crocodilians underwater in their fishing nets so that they cannot come up for air, and drown. In waterways that are used for recreation, such as angling, bathing and boating, crocodilians may be killed by the blades of a motorboat's engine and because they pose a threat to human life.

182

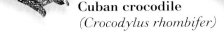

Cuban crocodile
(*Crocodylus rhombifer*)

◄ **CUBAN CROCODILE**
This crocodile has the smallest range of any living crocodilian and is seriously endangered. It lives only on the island of Cuba and the nearby Isle of Pines. The growth of charcoal burning has drastically reduced the habitat of the Cuban crocodile. It has also moved into coastal areas and rivers, where it is more in danger from hunters.

► **SIAMESE CROCODILE**
This endangered crocodile has almost died out in the wild. It was once found over large areas of South-east Asia, but wild Siamese crocodiles now live only in Thailand. They have become so rare because of extensive hunting and habitat destruction. They now survive mainly on crocodile farms.

▲ **ILLEGAL HUNTING**
This poacher has speared a caiman in the Brazilian rainforest. Hunting crocodilians is banned in many countries, but people still hunt illegally in order to make money. Their hides are so valuable that, even though this caiman's skin contains many bony scutes, it is still worthwhile taking the soft parts.

▼ **UNWANTED CROCODILE**
A small saltwater crocodile that strayed into somebody's garden is captured so it can be returned to the wild. Its jaws are bound together with rope to stop it biting the ranger. One of the biggest problems for crocodilians is the fact that more and more people want to live in the same places that they do.

Focus

WELL ADAPTED

Gharials have a light-coloured, slender body with extensive webbing between the toes on the back feet. Their long back legs are relatively weak. Gharials are well adapted for life in the water but are not fast swimmers.

The gharial of northern India and the false gharial of Southeast Asia are both endangered species. Their numbers have fallen due to hunting for their skins, habitat loss and competition for their main food, fish. Many of the fast-flowing rivers in which they live have been dammed to provide water for crops and to generate electricity. Dams flood some areas and reduce the flow of water in others, as well as damaging the river banks where gharials nest. People collect their eggs for food and believe them to have medicinal properties. To save the gharial, young are reared in captivity and released into the wild. The false gharial, however, does not breed well in captivity.

CAPTIVE SURVIVAL

This gharial was bred in captivity and has been released into the wild. It has a radio tag on its tail so that scientists can follow its movements. In the 1970s, there were only about 300 wild gharials left. Captive breeding has increased numbers to over 1,500.

MEAL TIME

A gharial lunges sideways to snap up a meal from a passing shoal of fish. Predatory catfish are a favourite meal. When gharial numbers went down, more catfish survived to eat the tilapia fish that local villagers caught for food.

on Gharials

FALSE IDENTITY

The false gharial looks like the true gharial and is probably related to it. It lives farther south than the true gharial, from southern Thailand to Borneo and Sumatra. In the wild, adults do not seem to help young escape from the nest and many die as they fend for themselves after hatching. Habitat loss and an increase in land used for rice farming have made false gharials rare. In Indonesia, over-collection of juveniles for rearing on farms may also have reduced numbers.

SAFE HOUSE

A scientist collects gharial eggs so that they can be protected in a sanctuary. There no predators will be able to get at them and the temperature can be kept just right for development. In the wild, about 40 per cent of eggs are destroyed by predators. Only about 1 per cent of the young survive to adulthood.

WATER SPORT

In the dry, low-water months of winter, gharials spend a lot of time basking on sand banks. Even so they are the most aquatic crocodilian. They move awkwardly when leaving the water and do not seem able to do the high walk like other crocodilians. Female gharials do not carry their young to the water. This is probably because their snouts are too slender and delicate and their teeth too sharp.

Conservation

Although people are frightened of crocodilians, they are a vital part of the web of life in tropical lands. They dig water holes that help other animals survive in dry seasons and clean up the environment by eating dead animals. Scientists find them interesting because they are good at fighting disease and rarely develop cancers. They are also fascinating to everyone as survivors from a prehistoric lost world. We need to find out more about their lives in the wild so we can help them to survive in the future. Some species, such as the American alligator, the saltwater crocodile and Johnston's crocodile of Australia and the gharial have already been helped by conservation measures. Much more work needs to be done, however, such as preserving their habitats, stopping illegal poaching and smuggling, breeding rare species in captivity and releasing them into the wild.

▲ **CROCODILE FARMS**
Tourists watch a wrestler show off his skill at a crocodile farm. The farm breeds crocodiles for their skins, attracting tourists as extra income. Farms help stop crocodiles being taken from the wild. The Samutprakan Crocodile Farm in Thailand has helped to save the rare Siamese crocodile from dying out by breeding them in captivity.

▶ **RESEARCH REFUGE**
Research at the Rockefeller Wildlife Refuge in Louisiana, USA, helped to work out the best way of rearing American alligators in captivity. They are brought up in special hothouses where temperature, humidity, diet, space and disease can be controlled. They have piped music so they will be less disturbed by outside noises. In these conditions, the alligators grow more than 1m a year – much faster than in the wild.

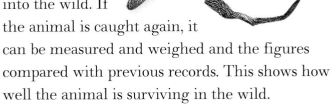

The tag on the foot of a black caiman helps identify it once it has been released into the wild. If the animal is caught again, it can be measured and weighed and the figures compared with previous records. This shows how well the animal is surviving in the wild.

▲ INTO THE FUTURE

This boy from Guyana is holding a baby dwarf caiman. Small numbers of caimans are sold as exotic pets. If people are paid more money for a living specimen than a dead one, they are less likely to kill crocodiles for skins. Educating people about why crocodilians are important is an important way of ensuring their future.

▶ RANCHING AND FARMING

A Nile crocodile is fed at a breeding station in South Africa. Crocodilians grow well on ranches or farms where they are fed properly. These places also provide information about the biology, health and feeding patterns of the reptiles.

◀ A NEW HOME

A row of black caimans, saved from a ranching scheme in Bolivia, wait to be flown to the Beni Biosphere Reserve, where they will be protected. The number of black caimans has dropped dramatically, and the animals they used to eat have increased as a result. This has caused problems for people, such as capybaras eating crops and piranhas attacking cattle.

SHARKS

Sharks are the swiftest, most powerful hunters of
the sea, and have evolved over millions of years
to become one of the world's most adept
predators. Descended from jawless fish, the shark
developed powerful jaws and teeth to become a
supreme hunter that devours many different
creatures, from plankton to seals, and
sometimes even humans.

Author: Michael Bright
Consultant: Ian K. Fergusson
The Shark Trust

What is a Shark?

There are about 400 different kinds of shark in the world. Some are as big as whales, others as small as a cigar. Whatever their size, they all eat meat. Some sharks eat tiny plants and animals called plankton. Others hunt down fish, squid, and even seals. Many sharks will also feed off the remains of another's meal or eat animal carcasses. They live at all depths, in every ocean, from tropical waters to cold polar seas. Some sharks can survive in the fresh water of rivers and lakes. Like other fish, sharks take oxygen from the water as it passes over their gills. Although some sharks like to live alone, others survive as part of a group.

▼ CLASSIC SHARK

This blue shark (*Prionace glauca*) is how most people imagine sharks. However, there are many different families of sharks in the seas and oceans and with a variety of body shapes.

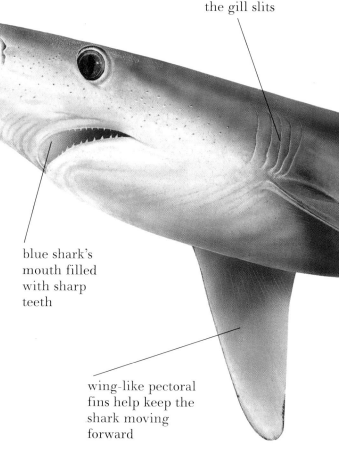

no cover over the gill slits

blue shark's mouth filled with sharp teeth

wing-like pectoral fins help keep the shark moving forward

◄ WHITE DEATH

The awesome great white shark (*Carcharodon carcharias*) is the largest hunting fish in the sea. It has an exaggerated reputation as a killer, partly because a killer shark appears in the film, *Jaws*. In reality great white sharks do often eat large prey, but they attack people only occasionally, in cases of mistaken identity.

▶ SHARK SCHOOL

Some sharks live alone, others live in schools (groups). Every day schools of female scalloped hammerhead sharks (*Sphyra lewini*) like these gather off the Mexican coast. At night, the sharks separate and hunt alone.

triangular dorsal (back) fin for stability

body packed with muscles for strength

▲ GENTLE GIANT

Although the basking shark (*Cetorhinus maximus*) is the second largest fish after the whale shark, it is not a hunter. It funnels water through its huge mouth, using gill rakers (giant combs) to filter out the tiny plankton that it eats.

flattened tail to help propel (push) through water

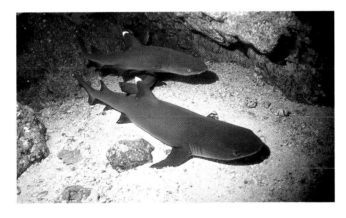

▲ REEF HUNTERS

Whitetip reef sharks (*Triaenodon obesus*) are one of the smaller species (kinds) of shark. They rarely grow over 2m long and hunt along tropical coral reefs at night.

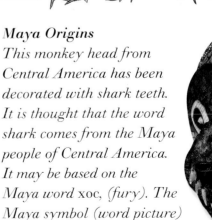

Maya Origins
This monkey head from Central America has been decorated with shark teeth. It is thought that the word shark comes from the Maya people of Central America. It may be based on the Maya word xoc, *(fury). The Maya symbol (word picture) for* xoc *is a shark-like creature.*

Shapes and Sizes

Many hunting sharks have long, rounded shapes, like the slim blue shark and the bulkier bull shark. Angel sharks have a flattened shape suited to hiding on the sea floor, while eel-like frilled sharks swim in the deep sea. Horn sharks have spines on their back, and megamouths (big mouths) have big, blubbery lips! As their names suggest, hammerhead sharks have hammer-shaped heads and sawsharks have elongated, saw-like snouts. Giant sharks, such as the whale shark, are as long as a school bus, and there are midget sharks, such as the Colombian lantern shark, which you could hold in the palm of your hand! Whatever the kind of shark, they are all perfectly adapted for the waters in which they live.

▲ GROTESQUE SHARK
The goblin shark (*Mitsukurina owstoni*) has an unusual, horn-shaped snout. This shark seems to have also lived in the dinosaur age. A fossil of a similar shark has been found in rocks that were created about 150 million years ago. Today, the goblin shark lives in very deep waters found off continental shelves.

▶ DEEP SEA NIPPER
The pygmy shark is one of the smallest sharks in the world. When fully grown, it is no more than 20cm long, making it smaller than a whale shark embryo (baby). It roams the gloomy waters of the Caribbean Sea, hunting in packs.

pygmy shark
(*Europtomicrus bispinatus*)

▲ STRANGE HEAD
The amazing heads of the hammerhead, bonnethead and winghead sharks are shaped like the letter T. These sharks use their hammers to detect prey and to aid swimming.

zebra bullhead shark
(*Heterodontus zebra*)

Did you know? The largest shark ever measured was 12.65m long.

▲ ROCK DISGUISE

Unlike many sharks, the spotted wobbegong shark (*Orectolobus maculatus*) has a flattened shape. It is a carpet shark (a family of camouflaged sharks that lie on the seabed), and disguises itself as part of the coral reef. The tassels under its mouth look like seaweed.

▲ SAFETY SPINES

A striped pattern helps the colourful zebra bullhead shark to camouflage itself (blend in) among corals and seaweed. For further protection, at the front of each dorsal fin is a sharp spine. If swallowed, the shark's spines will stick into the throat of any attacker, forcing it eventually to spit out its prickly meal.

► UNDERWATER TIGER

A young tiger shark has pale stripes along its body, which fade as it grows older. The powerful tiger shark (*Galeocerdo cuvier*) has a long, rounded shape, typical of hunting sharks. Some can rival great whites in size.

◄ BIG GULP

The whale shark (*Rhincodon typus*) is aptly named. Bigger than any other shark, it is closer in size to the giant whales. It is the largest fish in the sea, can grow to 12m in length and weigh up to 12 tonnes. With its giant mouth and large gill slits, the whale shark, like the basking shark, is a filter feeder.

Light and Strong

Although most fish are bony, the skeleton of a shark is made up almost entirely of cartilage, which is also found in the human nose. It is lighter and more elastic than bone, and it is this that makes the shark skeleton very flexible. This cartilage structure is strong enough to support a shark's huge muscles, and bendy enough to allow it to move with ease. Because sharks' skeleton cartilage and soft body parts decay (rot away) so quickly after they die, it is unusual to find complete shark fossils (preserved bodies) in ancient rocks. Only the hard teeth and spines are fossilized.

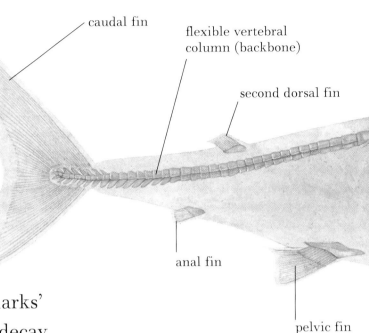

caudal fin

flexible vertebral column (backbone)

second dorsal fin

anal fin

pelvic fin

▼ PROTRUDING JAWS
A shark's jaws are attached to the skull by flexible ligaments. These allow some sharks to thrust their jaws forward when taking a bite.

teeth in upper jaw slice like a knife

▲ DARK TRIANGLE
Like the keel of a yacht, a shark's stiff dorsal fin helps it to balance in the water and stops it from slipping sideways. Most sharks have two dorsal fins, one at the front and one at the back, but some have just one.

▶ **AEROPLANE FINS**
A shark's pectoral fins,
one on each side, act like
the wings of an
aeroplane. As water
passes over them,
the fins give lift.

dorsal fin

gill arches
support
shark's gills

pectoral fin

compact
skull protects
brain and
nasal
capsules.

◀ **SHARK SKELETON**
The skeleton of a great white shark.
It is tough, flexible and typical of that
found in most sharks, providing support and
protection for the entire body. The great
white's muscles are attached to a long
backbone, the gills are supported by gill
arches and a box-like skull protects the brain.

▲ **CARTILAGE SOUP**
These fins have been cut from sharks and are
drying in the sun. The cartilage in a shark's
fin helps to make it stiff. When boiled in
water it makes a gluey substance that is used
in the Far East to make shark's fin soup.

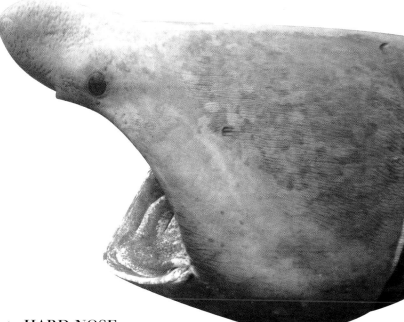

▶ **HARD NOSE**
The shark pictured above is an adult basking
shark. At birth, this shark has a strange, hooked
nose, like that of an elephant. When the
basking shark starts to grow, the cartilage in its
snout gradually straightens.

195

Tough Teeth

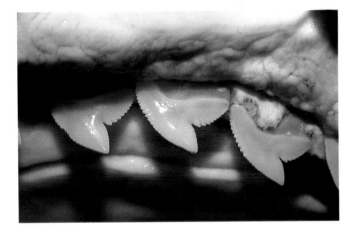

▲ SHARK SAW MASSACRE

The teeth of a tiger shark are shaped like the letter L. They can saw through skin, muscle and bone, and can even crack open the hard shell of a sea turtle. A tiger shark eats its prey by biting hard and shaking its head from side to side, slicing into its food like a chain saw.

▼ AWESOME JAWS

When it is about to grab its prey, a sandtiger shark opens and extends its awesome jaws. The rows of spiky teeth inside are perfect for grabbing and holding slippery fish and squid. Once caught, the prey is swallowed whole.

sandtiger shark
(*Eugomphodus taurus*)

A shark species can be identified by the shape of its teeth alone. Each species has its own distinctive shape, designed for the type of food it eats. Some have sharp, spiky teeth that can hold on to slippery fish and squid. Others have broad, grinding teeth that can crack open shellfish. The teeth of some species of shark change as they get older and hunt different prey. Although sharks lose their teeth regularly, the teeth are always replaced. Behind each row of teeth lie more rows. If a front tooth is dislodged, an extra tooth simply moves forward to take its place!

▲ NEEDLE POINT

This 2m-long leopard shark (*Triakis semifasciata*) has rows of small, needle-sharp, teeth. Although it is thought to be harmless, in 1955 a leopard shark sunk its tiny teeth into a skin diver in Trinidad Bay, California. This was an unprovoked attack, and the diver escaped.

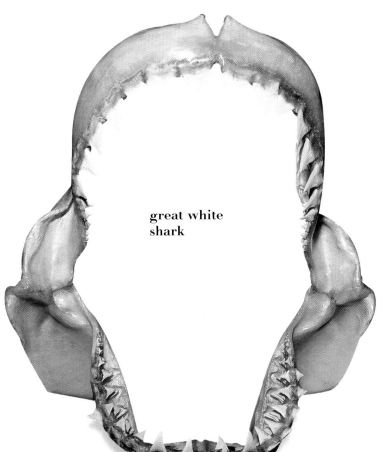

great white
shark

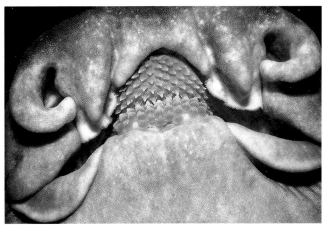

▲ DUAL SETS OF TEETH
The Port Jackson shark (*Heterodontus portusjacksoni*) has small, sharp teeth for catching small fish and broad, crushing teeth that can crack open shellfish.

▼ BIG TEETH
The cookie-cutter is a small shark, reaching only 50cm long. However, for its body size, it has the biggest teeth of any shark known. It uses them to cut round chunks out of its prey, which includes dolphins, whales and large fish.

▲ JAWS
The awesome
jaws of a great white
shark are filled with two types of teeth. The upper jaw is lined with large, triangular teeth that can slice through flesh. The lower jaw contains long, pointed teeth that are used to hold and slice prey.

cookie-
cutter shark
(*Isistius
brasiliensis*)

Shark Man
Ceremonial carvings such as this one were used in ritual dances performed in the South Pacific Solomon Islands. From one dance master to another, these traditional dances were handed down through many generations. They told of myths in which sharks turned into men, and men turned back into sharks again.

Shark Bodies

Sharks are incredible machines, packed with muscle. Some sharks, such as the great white and mako, can even keep their muscles, gut, brain, and eyes warmer than the temperature of the seawater around them. They do this with special blood vessels, which work like a radiator to collect the heat in the blood and send it back into the body. These make muscles more efficient, allowing the sharks to swim faster. They also help these sharks to hunt in seas of different temperatures. Sharks have a huge, oil-filled liver that helps to keep them afloat. However, like an aeroplane, they must also move forwards in order to stay up. Open ocean sharks must swim all the time, not only to stop them from sinking, but also to breathe. Some sharks can take a rest on the seabed by pumping water over their gills to breathe.

▲ **GILL BREATHERS**
Like this sixgill shark (*Hexanchus griseus*), most sharks breathe by taking oxygen-rich water into their mouths. The oxygen passes into the blood and the water exits the gill slits.

▲ **OCEAN RACER**
The shortfin mako shark (*Isurus oxyrinchus*) is the fastest shark in the sea. Using special, warm muscles, it can travel at speeds of 35–50 kph and catch fast-swimming swordfish.

◄ **SUSPENDED ANIMATION**
The sandtiger shark (*Eugomphodus taurus*) can hold air in its stomach. The air acts like a life jacket, helping the shark to hover in the water. Sandtiger sharks stay afloat without moving, lurking among rocks and caves.

► KEEP MOVING

Like many hunting sharks, the grey reef shark (*Carcharinhus amblyrynchos*) cannot breathe unless it moves forwards. The forward motion passes oxygen into its gills. If it stops moving, the shark will drown.

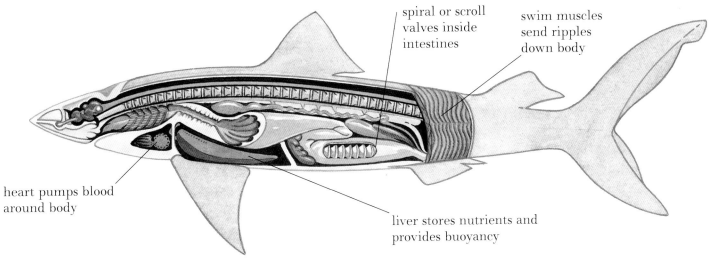

spiral or scroll valves inside intestines

swim muscles send ripples down body

heart pumps blood around body

liver stores nutrients and provides buoyancy

▲ INSIDE A SHARK

If you could look inside a shark, you would find thick muscles, an enormous liver, an intestine with a special, spiral valve, and a complicated system of blood vessels that supply the shark's gills.

Did you know? Mako sharks have been seen to leap 6m clear of the water.

◄ ABLE TO REST

The tawny nurse shark (*Nebrius ferrugineus*) pumps water over its gills by lifting the floor of its mouth. This allows it to rest on the seabed, yet still breathe. Whitetip reef sharks, lemon sharks, catsharks and nursehounds also do this.

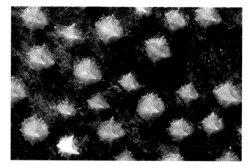
skin teeth of Greenland shark

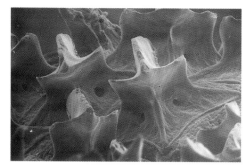
skin teeth of spiny dogfish

skin teeth of dusky shark

▲ SKIN TEETH

A shark's skin is covered with tiny skin teeth called dermal denticles. These teeth help to speed the shark through the water by controlling the flow of water over its body.

▶ STREAMLINED SHARK

The upper part of the grey reef shark's tail is slightly larger than the lower. Because of this, the tail's downward movement is so powerful that it balances the lift from the pectoral wings. Scientists believe that this helps the shark to move evenly through the water.

Wings in Water

A shark has two pairs of fins (pectoral and pelvic) that work like an aeroplane's wings, lifting the shark as it moves forward. Its dorsal fins and anal fin stop it from rolling sideways, like the tail fin of an aircraft. A shark moves forward in an S shape by rippling a series of waves down its entire body. These waves increase in size as they reach the shark's tail, helping it to propel the body forwards. The shape of the tail can vary from shark to shark, depending on the area of water it inhabits. Sharks that live at the bottom of the sea, such as the nurse shark, tend to have large, flat tails. Sharks that swim in open oceans, such as the tiger shark, usually have slimmer, more curved tails. Both types have a larger upper part to their tail. Sharks that stalk and dash to catch their prey, such as the great white and mako shark, have crescent-shaped tails with top and bottom parts the same size.

▲ SEABED SWIMMERS

Hammerhead sharks have unusually small pectoral fins, which allow them to swim and feed close to the seabed. The wings of the hammer-shaped head give the shark extra lift in the water and allow it to turn very tightly. Hammerhead sharks are very adaptable and skilful hunters.

▲ DEEP SEA GIANT

The megamouth shark (*Megachasma pelagios*) was only discovered in 1976. It lives in deep water and swims very slowly. Megamouth does not chase anything. It eats deep-sea shrimps filtered through its gills.

▲ OCEAN TRAVELLER

The blue shark (*Prionace glauca*) has long pectoral fins that help it to sail through the sea like a glider plane, making long journeys easy. It swims to the surface, then glides effortlessly to the depths before swimming back to the surface again.

▲ OCEAN CRUISER

The oceanic whitetip shark (*Carcharhinus longimanus*) swims in the open oceans and is often present at the scene of sea disasters. It is a very distinctive shark, and can be easily recognized by its dorsal and pectoral fins, which are shaped like rounded garden spades.

Brain and Senses

A shark's brain is small for its size, but its senses are highly developed. Sharks see well, and see in colour. They can also recognize shapes. Just as amazing are a different range of senses that allow sharks to pick up sounds and vibrations from miles around. They can detect changes in the ocean currents, recognize smells and follow the trail of an odour right back to its source. Some species have shiny plates at the backs of their eyes that collect light to help them see as they dive to deep, dark water. They also have membranes of dark colour that they draw across the shiny plates to avoid being dazzled by the light when they return to the surface. Sharks even have special nerves in their noses that can detect minute electrical fields, such as those produced by the muscles of their prey.

▲ **ELECTRICAL SENSE**
Like all sharks, sandtiger sharks have tiny pits in their snouts, known as the ampullae of Lorenzini. Inside these pits are special nerves. These help the shark to find food by detecting minute electrical fields in the muscles of its prey.

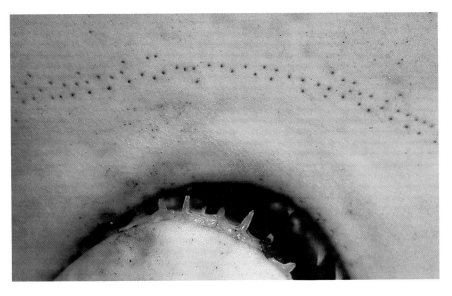

◄ **PREY DETECTOR**
In a hammerhead shark the special pits that can sense electrical fields in its prey are spread across the hammer of the shark's head, helping it to scan for prey across a wide area. The hammerhead searches for food by sweeping its head from side to side, rather as if using a metal detector. It can find any prey buried in the sand below.

◄ SIGHT, SMELL AND SOUND

The nostrils of the hammerhead shark are positioned wide apart on its head. This gives the shark 'stereo smelling' with which it can more easily track odours to their source. But, because its eyes are at the ends of its hammer, it must turn its head from side to side in order to see forwards.

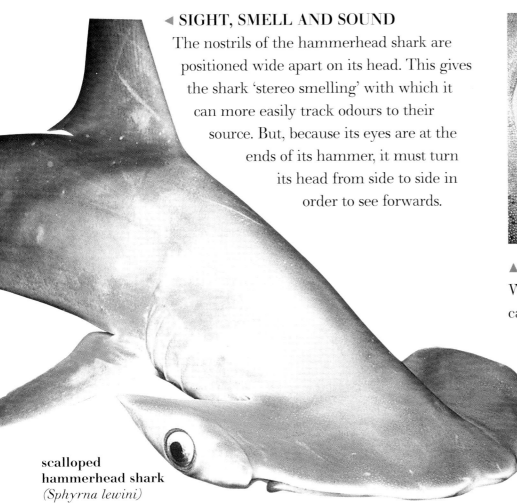

scalloped
hammerhead shark
(*Sphyrna lewini*)

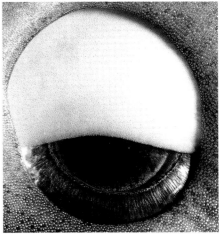

▲ EYE PROTECTION

When a shark bites, its eyes can easily be injured by the victim's teeth, spines or claws. To prevent this, sharks such as this tiger shark have a special membrane (sheath) that slides down across the eye during the attack.

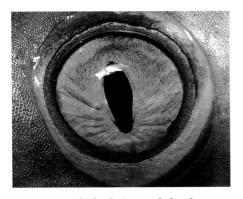

eye of blacktip reef shark
(*Carcharhinus melanopterus*)

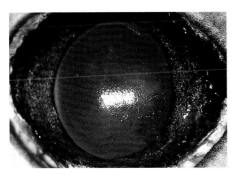

eye of bluntnose sixgill shark
(*Hexanchus griseus*)

◄ DEEP AND SHALLOW

The blacktip reef shark has a small eye with a narrow, vertical slit. This type of eye is often found in shallow-water sharks. Sharks that swim in deeper waters, such as the sixgill shark, tend to have large, round pupils.

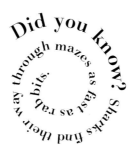

Did you know? Sharks find their way through mazes as fast as rabbits.

Shark Callers
On the islands of the south-west Pacific, sharks are the islanders' gods. To test their manhood, young shark callers attract sharks by shaking a coconut rattle under the water. Sensing the vibrations, a shark will swim close to the canoe. It is then wrestled into the boat, and its meat divided among the villagers as a gift from the gods.

Focus on the Blue

The blue shark is an open ocean hunter. Continually looking for food, it can pick up the sounds and vibrations of a struggling fish from over a kilometre away. From half a kilometre, it can smell blood and other body fluids in the water. As it gets closer, the shark can sense changes in the water that help it locate moving prey. Finally, vision takes over. First, only movements are seen, but then the prey itself. As the blue shark closes in for the kill, it pulls down its eye protectors and swims blind. Its electrical sensors then lead it to its prey.

2 Smells, sounds, vibrations, and water movements attract the blue shark. The movements made by a school of jack mackerel will initially lead the shark to them. It then uses its sight to find an easy target.

1 When hunting, the blue shark uses all its senses to search constantly the ocean ahead for prey. It will also watch the behaviour of other blue sharks in the water, sometimes joining them to hunt in packs.

Shark Hunt

3 Sharp eyesight, quick reactions and an ability to speed through the water all help the blue shark to chase its chosen target. In an attempt to escape, this group of mackerel fish will dart all over the place, then crowd close together to confuse the pursuing shark.

4 As the blue shark closes in to grab its target, a protective membrane covers each eye. At this stage the shark is swimming blind and relies on the electrical sensors in its snout to guide it to its prey. These home in on the electrical field made by the fish's muscles, leading the shark for the last few centimetres.

5 As the shark bites, it extends its jaws and impales its prey on the teeth of the lower jaw. Next, the upper jaw teeth come into action, clamping down on the fish. The shark then removes its lower jaw teeth from the prey, and pushes them forward to pull the fish back into its mouth. The prey is then swallowed by the shark.

Feeding

Sharks catch a variety of foods, eating whatever they can find in their area. Most sharks eat bony fish and squid, but they can be cannibalistic (eat each other). They often feed on other smaller sharks, sometimes even on their own species. Some sharks prefer particular kinds of food. Hammerheads like sting rays, while tiger sharks will crunch a sea turtle's shell for the meat inside. Shortfin mako sharks hunt bluefish and swordfish. Great white sharks eat fish, but as they get older will also hunt seals and sea lions. Sharks will scavenge (feed on dead animals) whenever they can. The bodies of dead whales are food for many sharks that swim in open waters, including tigers, blues and oceanic whitetips.

▲ **FEEDING FRENZY**
Large quantities of food will excite grey reef sharks, sending them into a feeding frenzy. When divers hand out food, the sharks will circle with interest, until one darts forward for the first bite. Other sharks quickly follow, grabbing at the food until they seem out of control.

▲ **FOREVER EATING**
A large shoal of mating squid will send blue sharks into a frenzy. The sharks feed until full, then empty their stomachs to start again!

▲ **FISH BALL**
A group of sharks will often herd shoals of fish into a tight ball. The sharks will then pick off fish from the outside of the ball, one by one.

▶ BITE A BROTHER

Sharks do not look after their relatives!
Big sharks will often eat smaller sharks,
and sharks that swim side-by-side in the
same school will often take a nip out of
each other. The
remains caught on
a fishing line of
this blacktip
shark show that it
has been eaten by
a large bull shark.

Did you know? The great white shark sometimes eats crabs and lobsters.

◀ OCEAN DUSTBIN

Tiger sharks are well known as
the sharks that will eat not just
living things such as fish, other
sharks, or dead animals floating
in the sea. Tiger sharks have
been known to eat coal, rubber
tyres and clothes. They are found
all over the world and grow to a
length of 5.5m. Not surprisingly,
tiger sharks have been known to
try eating humans.

▼ BITE-SIZE CHUNKS

The cookie-cutter shark feeds by
cutting chunks out of whales and
dolphins, such as this spinner dolphin.
The shark uses its mouth like a
clamp, attaching itself to its
victim. It then bites
with its razor-sharp
teeth and swivels to
twist off a circle
of flesh.

spinner dolphin
(Stenella longirostris)

▲ OPPORTUNISTS

Sharks will often follow fishing
boats, looking for a free meal.
This silvertip shark is eating
pieces of tuna fish that have
been thrown overboard.

Focus on

1 Huge groups of albatrosses nest on the ground close to the shore of Hawaiian islands, including the island of Laysan. The birds in each group breed, nest, and hatch their babies at the same time. When it is time, the young birds all take their first flight within days of each other.

Sharks can be found wherever there is food in or near the sea. Tiger sharks are rarely seen around some Hawaiian islands in the Pacific Ocean until the islands' young seabirds start to fly. Then the sharks arrive. Any birds that fall into the sea are quickly eaten. The waters are too shallow for the sharks to attack from behind and below as most sharks do. Instead, the sharks leap clear of the surface then drag the birds underwater to drown and eat them. Sharks arrive for their island feast at the same time each year. How they remember to do so is yet to be explained.

2 When ready to fly, a baby bird practises by flapping its wings in the face of the islands' fierce winds. Eventually, the baby must make its first real flight over the ocean. When it does so, the tiger sharks are waiting in the water below.

3 Tiger sharks patrol the clear, shallow waters close to the albatross nests. Their dark shapes can be seen clearly against the sandy sea floor. Every now and again, a tiger shark's triangular dorsal fin and the tip of its tail can be seen breaking the water's surface.

Tiger Sharks

4 Any baby bird that dips into the sea is prey for the waiting tiger shark. At first, the shark tries its usual attack, from below and behind. However, in the shallow waters the shark cannot make a full attack. Rather than hitting its prey at force, the shark just pushes the bird away on the wave made by its snout.

5 After failing to catch a meal, the shark soon realizes its mistake and tries another approach. Its next style of attack is to shoot across the surface of the water, slamming into its target with its mouth wide open. This technique seems to be more successful, and the shark usually catches the bird.

6 The shark then attempts to drag the bird below the surface, to drown it. If a bird is pushed ahead on the shark's bow wave, it will bravely peck at its attacker's broad snout and, sometimes, may even escape. Some birds also manage to wriggle free as the shark grapples with them underwater.

7 Many albatross babies do not manage to escape a shark attack. They are grabbed by the sharks and drowned. Inside the tiger shark's jaws are rows of sharp teeth that can slice into a bird's body like a saw. Sometimes the tiger shark tears off the bird's wings and leaves them aside to eat the body whole.

Filter Feeders

Some of the biggest fish in the sea eat some of the smallest living things there. Giant species, like the whale shark and basking shark, use their gill rakers to comb plankton (tiny animals and plants) from the water. In the same way as hunting sharks, they use their sharp senses to track down huge areas of food. Whale sharks are often seen near coral reefs, where, at certain times of the year, large amounts of animal plankton can be found. Basking sharks often swim in the area between ocean currents, feeding on plankton that gathers on the boundary. Whale and basking sharks swim in the upper layers of the sea. The giant megamouth shark lives deeper down, sieving out the shrimps that live in the middle layers of the ocean.

▲ FOOD CHAIN

Eggs and sperm released on the same night by the corals of the Ningaloo Reef in Australia are eaten by the larvae (young) of crabs and lobsters. The larvae are eaten by fish and krill. The fish and krill in turn become food for the hungry whale sharks that swim off the coral reefs.

◀ WHALE OF A FEAST

Exactly two weeks after the coral has spawned at Ningaloo, the whale sharks appear. By this time, each creature, from the smallest larvae to the reef's fish and krill, will have fed upon the coral's rich food. Each night, the whale sharks swim with their huge mouths wide open, scooping up food which they sieve from the sea's surface.

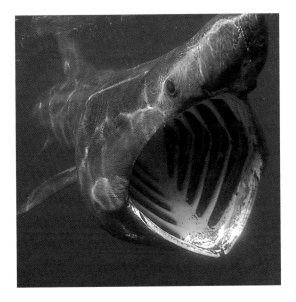

▲ BIG GULP

The basking shark swims slowly through the sea, funnelling food-filled water into its great mouth. In one hour, it can filter 7,000 litres of seawater! When enough food has been trapped, the shark closes its mouth and swallows with one gulp.

▲ COLD WATER SKIMMERS

The basking shark has gill slits that almost encircle its gigantic body. These are used to filter food, such as shellfish larvae and fish eggs, from the water. The shark passes water through its gill chamber, where enormous gill rakers comb the food from the water.

▲ PLANKTON

Plankton is made up of tiny plants and animals that float together in huge clouds on and just below the sea's surface. Both animal and plant plankton are eaten by the basking shark.

▲ BIG MOUTH

Patrolling the middle waters of the deep, the megamouth shark scoops up tiny shrimps as they cross its path. Since this shark's discovery in 1976, a further 13 examples have been discovered and some of these have been examined by scientists.

Keep in Line

No shark is alone for long. Sooner or later, one shark will come across another, including those of its own kind. In order to reduce the risk of fights and injury, sharks talk to each other, not with sound, but with body language. Sharks have a clear pecking order. The bigger the shark, the more important it is. Not surprisingly, small sharks tend to keep out of the way of larger ones. Many species use a sign that tells others to keep their distance. They arch their back, point their pectoral fins down and swim stiffly. If this doesn't work, the offending shark will be put in its place with a swift bite to the sides or head. Bite marks along its gill slits can be a sign that a shark has stepped out of line and been told firmly to watch out.

▲ GREAT WHITE CHUMS
Great white sharks were once thought to travel alone, but it is now known that some journey in pairs or small groups. Some sharks that have been identified by scientists will appear repeatedly at favourite sites, such as California's Farallon Islands, 42km off the coast of San Francisco. There they lie in wait for seals.

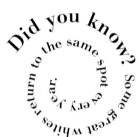

Did you know? Some great whites return to the same spot every year.

◄ BED FELLOWS
Sharks, like these whitetip reef sharks, will snooze alongside each other on the seabed. They search for a safe place to rest below overhanging rocks and coral, where, as fights rarely break out, they seem to tolerate each other. The sharks remain here until dusk, when they separate to hunt.

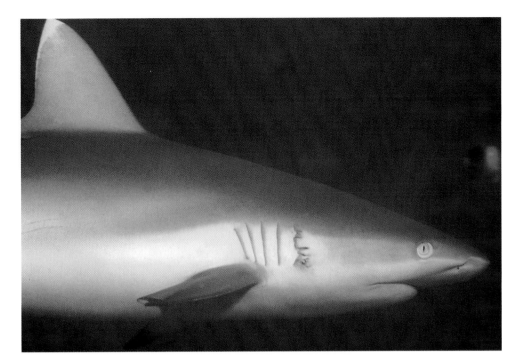

◄ PECKING ORDER

This grey reef shark has swum too close to another, larger shark and has been bitten on its gill slits as a punishment. The marks on its skin show that its attacker raked the teeth of its lower jaw across the sensitive skin of the grey reef's gill slits. A shark's injuries heal rapidly, so this unfortunate victim will recover quickly from its wounds.

► REEF SHARK GANGS

Sharks have their own personal space. As they patrol the edge of a reef, schools of blacktip reef sharks will tell others that they are too close by moving their jaw or opening their mouth. During feeding, order sometimes breaks down and a shark might be injured in the frenzy.

◄ SHARK SCHOOL

Every day schools of scalloped hammerhead sharks gather close to underwater mountains in the Pacific Ocean. They do not feed, even though they come across shoals of fish that would normally be food. Instead, they swim repeatedly up and down, as though taking a rest.

213

Focus on

By day scalloped hammerhead sharks swim in large schools around underwater volcanoes in the Pacific, the Gulf of California off Mexico, and off the Coco and Galapagos islands. This species of shark cannot stop swimming or it will drown. Schools are a safe resting place for them. Even sharks have enemies, such as other sharks and killer whales, so there is safety in numbers. In schools, scalloped hammerheads can also find a mate. At night, they separate to hunt. They swim to favourite feeding sites, using their electric sensors to follow magnetic highways made by lava on the seabed.

BAD-TEMPERED SHARKS

The larger a female hammerhead becomes, the less likely she is to get on with her neighbours! Older and larger hammerhead sharks like more space than smaller, younger sharks. In hammerhead schools, the relationship between sharks seems to be controlled by constant displays of threat and small fights.

FEMALES ONLY

The sharks in this huge school of hammerheads are mainly females. Larger sharks swim in the centre, and smaller sharks on the outside. Large sharks dominate the group, choosing the best positions in which to swim. Not only is the middle safer, but it is also the place where male sharks look for a mate.

Hammerheads

READY FOR A SCRUB

At some gathering sites, such as Cocos Island in the eastern Pacific, sharks drop out of the school and swoop down to cleaning stations close to the reef. From the reef, butterfly fish dart out to eat the dead skin and irritating parasites that cling to the outside of the shark's body.

BODY LANGUAGE

Larger sharks within a school perform strange movements and dances to keep smaller sharks in their place. At the end of the movement, a large shark may nip a smaller one on the back of the head!

STRANGE HEAD

The scalloped hammerhead is so named because of the groove at the front of its head, which gives it a scalloped (scooped out) appearance. The black tips on the underside of its pectoral fins are another way of identifying this particular shark.

Courtship and Mating

Male sharks find female sharks by their smell. The female gives off odours that drift in the currents of the sea, attracting every male shark within smelling distance. The males follow her closely, until one grabs hold of a pectoral fin with his mouth and hangs on tightly in preparation for mating. Fortunately, the female has thickened skin on her pectoral fins, which prevents her from being hurt. The male has a pair of claspers (sex organs) one of which he places inside the female's sexual opening. During mating, the male shark shakes occasionally, to make sure that the female accepts his presence. Once he is sure of this, the male will complete his mating with her.

▲ **ENGAGEMENT IN THE SHALLOWS**
A group of male whitetip sharks will be stimulated by the sexual smell of a female ready to mate. Following her in the shallow waters of a coral reef, the males compete for the female. Eventually, one will win possession by grabbing hold of one of her pectoral fins.

◄ **HANGING AROUND**
Sandtiger sharks hover in the water at special meeting places, waiting for members of the opposite sex. At these sites, lots of shark teeth are found on the sea floor. It is believed that they fall out during the rough and tumble of courtship and mating.

◄ THREE IS A CROWD

Male sharks are usually smaller than females of the same age. Here two males have each seized a female's pectoral fin, but only one male will be able to mate with her.

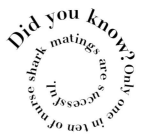

Did you know? Only one in ten of nurse shark matings are successful.

► NURSE SHARK NUPTIALS

Nurse sharks (*Ginglymostoma cirratum*) travel to traditional mating sites. The male nurse shark grips the female's pectoral fin and arches his body alongside hers. He will then insert his right or left clasper, depending on which pectoral fin he has seized.

▲ MALE SEX ORGANS

The claspers (sex organs) of male sharks are pelvic fins that have been adapted for mating. Similar to the penises of mammals, they are used to transfer sperm from the male into the female.

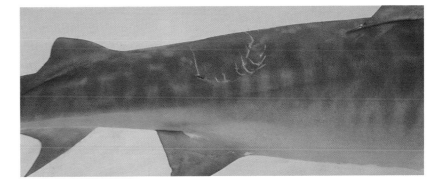

▲ MATING SCARS

The courtship and mating of sharks can be a rough affair. Female sharks, like this tiger shark, can be scarred with bite marks made by her mate. However, females have thicker skin than males, which prevents further damage.

Inside and Outside

▲ **EGG WITH A TWIST**
The horn shark (*Heterodontus francisci*) egg case has a spiral-shaped ridge. The mother shark uses her mouth like a screwdriver to twist the case round into the gaps in rocks.

Sharks bring their young into the world in two ways. Most sharks grow their eggs inside the mother's body, and give birth to breathing young called pups. Others lay eggs in which the pup grows outside of the mother's body. Catsharks and nursehound sharks grow their young in cases called mermaid's purses, which they lay outside their bodies. These can sometimes be found washed up on beaches after a storm. Each mating season, catsharks lay up to 20 mermaid's purses. Inside each is one pup. When the case has been laid in the sea, the mother shark does not guard or look after it in any way. Instead, she relies on the tough, leathery case to protect the pup inside.

▲ **TIME TO LEAVE**
When it is ready to leave its egg, the baby horn shark uses special scales on its snout and pectoral fins to cut its way out of the tough egg case. On its dorsal fins are tough spines that protect it from the moment it emerges.

Mermaid's Purses
The mermaid is a mythical undersea creature with a woman's body and a fish's tail. In legends, the mermaid lured men to their death with beautiful songs. Catshark and skate cases that are washed up on beaches look like pouches, and are often called mermaid's purses.

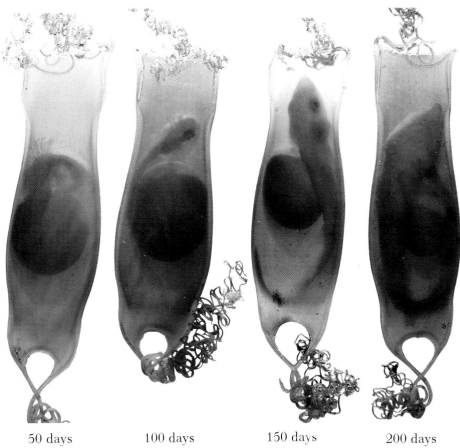

50 days   100 days   150 days   200 days

▲ IN THE SAC

In the earliest stages of development, the catshark pup is tiny. It is attached to a huge, yellow yolk sac from which it takes its food. Inside the egg case, the growing catshark pup makes swimming movements, which keeps the egg fluids and supply of oxygen fresh. After nine months, the pup emerges, with diagonal stripes that eventually turn into spots as it grows.

► SWELL SHARK

The length of time it takes the swell shark (*Cephaloscyllium ventriosum*) pup to grow depends on the temperature of the sea water around it. If warm, it can take just seven months. If cold, it might take ten months. As it emerges, it uses special skin teeth to tear its capsule open.

Into the World

Most sharks give birth to fully formed, breathing pups. However, pups grow in many different ways. Baby nurse and whale sharks start their life in small capsules. The pups then hatch from the capsules inside their mother's body, where they continue to grow before being born. Other shark pups, like blue sharks, also grow inside their mothers, in a womb. A sandtiger shark might have just two pups, but a blue shark can grow up to 135 at one time. The length of time it takes a pup to grow also varies. Nurse sharks take just five months, but frilled sharks take two years. Some pups feed on unfertilized eggs inside the womb. Baby sandtiger sharks go one better. They eat each other.

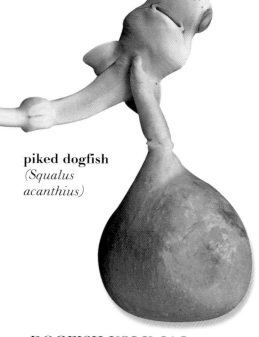

piked dogfish
(*Squalus acanthius*)

▲ **DOGFISH YOLK SAC**
Up to 12 piked dogfish pups can grow inside one mother. At first, all the pups are enclosed in one capsule that breaks after six months. Each pup then feeds off its own yolk sac until it is born three months later.

▶ **RESTING**
When birth is near, a pregnant whitetip reef shark will rest in a protective area. This pregnant shark is resting on rocks near Cocos Island in the Pacific. Inside her womb, she may develop up to five pups. Each will be fed by a placenta attached to the womb wall.
The pups are born after five months.

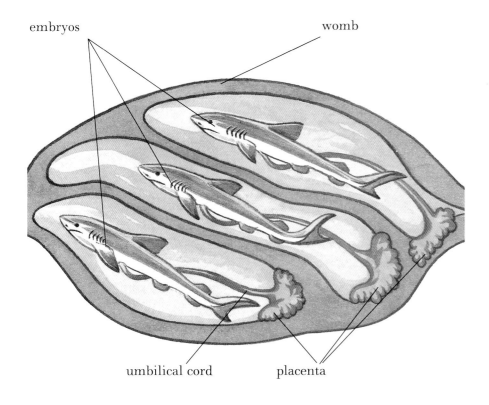

embryos　　　　　　　　　　womb

umbilical cord　　　　placenta

▲ WOMB MATES

In some species of shark, such as the whaler shark, embryos develop inside the pregnant female as they do in mammals. At first, each embryo has its own supply of food in a yolk sac, but when this is used up its sac turns into a placenta that attaches itself to the wall of the womb. Nutrients and oxygen pass directly from the mother across the placenta and along the umbilical cord to its own body. Waste products go the other way.

▲ BIG BELLIES

Some baby sharks will eat unfertilized eggs in their mothers' wombs. They eat so much so fast their stomachs become swollen. These baby shortfin mako sharks, caught off the coast of South Africa, have gorged on unfertilized eggs, filling their tiny stomachs.

◄ STRIPED SHARK

Safe inside its mother, this baby tiger shark will have fed on both the nutrients from its yolk sac, and on a fluid produced by the wall of the womb. The pattern of blotches on the newborn baby's skin will form stripes, which will gradually fade as it gets older.

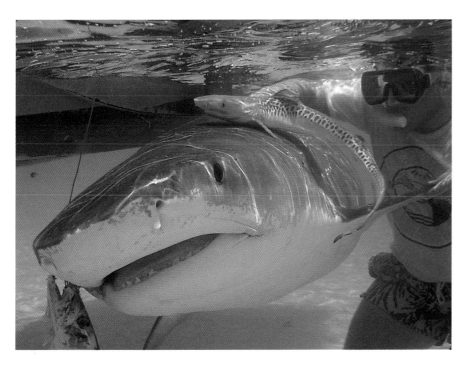

Focus on Lemon

A year after mating, pregnant lemon sharks arrive at Bimini Island in the Atlantic Ocean. Here, they give birth to their pups in the island's shallow lagoon where males do not enter. An adult male is quite likely to eat a smaller shark, even one of its own kind. In many species of shark, pregnant female sharks leave the males and swim to safer nursery areas to give birth. Some scientists even believe that females lose their appetite at pupping time, to avoid eating their own young. After birth, however, the lemon shark pups live on their own.

1 By pumping sea water over her gills, a pregnant lemon shark (*Negaprion brevirostris*) can breathe and rest on the seabed at Bimini Island. She gives birth on the sandy lagoon floor to the pups that have developed inside her for a year.

2 Baby lemon sharks are born tail first. There might be 5–17 pups in a mother's litter (family). Each pup is about 60cm long. After her litter is born, a female lemon shark will not be able to mate again straight away. Instead, she will rest for a year.

Shark Birth

3 A female lemon shark can give birth to her pups as she swims slowly through the shallows. The pups are still attached to the umbilical cord when born, but a sharp tug soon releases them. The small remora fish that follow the shark everywhere will feast on the afterbirth.

4 After birth, a baby lemon shark makes for the safety of the mangroves at the edge of the lagoon. Here, it spends the first few years of its life in a strip of mangrove 40m wide and 400m long feeding on small fish, worms and shellfish, taking care to avoid sharks larger than itself. Its home overlaps the territory of other young sharks.

5 To avoid being eaten, young lemon sharks gather with others of the same size. Each group patrols its own section of the lagoon at Bimini. This young lemon shark is about one year old. When it is seven or eight, it will leave the safety of the lagoon and head for the open reefs outside.

Look in any Ocean

Sharks live throughout the world's oceans and seas, and at all depths. Some sharks, like bull sharks, even swim in rivers and lakes. Whale, reef and nurse sharks are all tropical species that prefer warm waters. Temperate-water sharks, such as the mako, horn and basking sharks, live in water that is 10–20°C. Cold-water sharks often live in very deep water. The Portuguese shark, frilled shark, and goblin shark are all cold water sharks. A few species will swim in extremely cold waters, such as the Greenland shark which braves the icy water around the Arctic Circle.

NORTH
AMERICA

PACIFIC
OCEAN

ATLA
OC▶

SOUTH
AMERICA

▶ **SWIMMING POOLS**

This map shows the main parts of the world's seas in which different kinds of sharks live. The key beneath the map shows which sharks live where.

▶ **OCEAN WANDERER**

The oceanic whitetip shark swims the world's deep, open oceans, in tropical and sub-tropical waters. It is also one of the first sharks to appear at shipwrecks.

KEY

whale shark

basking shark

bull shark

tiger shark

whitetip shark

Greenland shark

great white shark

◀ **ISLAND LIVING**

The Galapagos shark (*Carcharhinus galapagensis*) swims in the waters of the Galapagos islands, on the Equator. It also swims around tropical islands in the Pacific, Atlantic and Indian oceans.

◄ UNDER THE ICE

The Greenland shark (*Somniosus microcephalus*) is the only shark known to survive under polar ice in the North Atlantic seas. It has a luminous parasite attached to each eye that attracts prey to the area around its mouth.

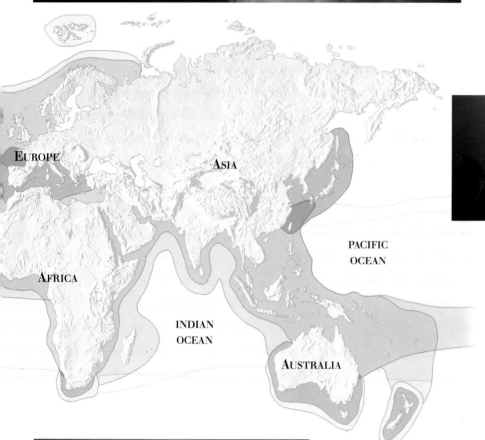

EUROPE
ASIA
AFRICA
PACIFIC OCEAN
INDIAN OCEAN
AUSTRALIA

▲ TEMPERATE PREDATOR

The great white shark lives in temperate, sub-tropical and tropical seas, including the Mediterranean. It usually swims in coastal waters rather than the open sea.

▲ TIGER OF THE SEAS

The tiger shark swims in mainly tropical and warm temperate waters, both in open ocean, and close to shore. Tiger sharks have been seen off Morocco and the Canary Islands.

◄ REEF SHARK

The blacktip reef shark patrols reefs in the Indian and Pacific oceans. It also lives in the Mediterranean and Red Sea, and as far west as the seas off Tunisia, in North Africa.

225

Upwardly Mobile

Not all sharks travel far afield. Some prefer to stay close to home, swimming only in one small area. Others have a daily routine, spending the day in deep waters, but moving closer to shore to feed at night. A few deep sea sharks make a different daily journey, spending the day in the deep, and rising to the surface to feed at night. Some sharks travel vast distances, crossing oceans. This has only recently been discovered with the tagging of sharks. Rather than killing sharks when they catch them, scientists and fishermen now give them a special tag. Each tag has its own number, which identifies the shark. So, when the shark is caught again, scientists can see how much it has grown, and also how far it has travelled.

sandbar shark
(*Carcharinus plumbeus*)

Did you know? A blue shark once travelled a total distance of 7,146 km.

▲ **INTO THE GULF**
Atlantic sandbar sharks can travel over 3,000km, from the Atlantic coastline of the USA to the coast of Mexico. These amazing sharks grow incredibly slowly, only about 3cm a year. They reach adulthood very late in life, when they are 30 years old.

◄ **GIVEN A NAME**
This tiger shark has been tagged (marked) by scientists and is being released back into the sea. Tagging has shown that tiger sharks travel great distances across oceans. Previously people had believed that they stayed in one place.

◀ **OCEAN MIGRATOR**
Female blue sharks in the North Atlantic go on a very long migration. They circle the Atlantic Ocean, mating off North America and then giving birth near Spain and Portugal at the end of their journey.

▶ **EPIC JOURNEY**
Female blue sharks travel from North America to Europe where they give birth to their pups. Then they turn back towards the USA. They travel at about 40 km per day. A shark swimming fast might cover the round trip of 15,000km in 15 months.

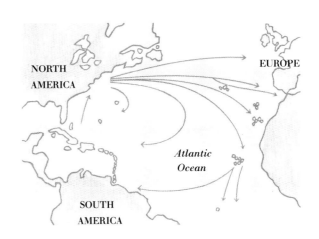

▼ **FOLLOW THE TEMPERATURE**
Shortfin mako sharks travel into the North Atlantic, but rarely swim the whole way across. They like to swim in an exact temperature of 17–22°C. They follow thermal water corridors through the ocean to winter in the Sargasso Sea.

shortfin mako shark
(Isurus oxyrinchus)

▶ **DOUBLE BACK**
Migrating mako sharks travel to the middle of the Atlantic Ocean and then turn back towards the USA. The sharks do not go further because from the middle of the ocean to Europe the water is not the temperature they prefer to swim in.

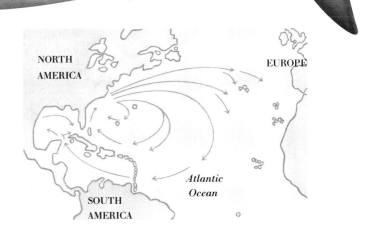

227

frilled shark
(Chlamydoselachus anguineus)

The Ocean Depths

Many sharks are rarely seen because they live in the darkness of the deep. Catsharks and dogfish live in these gloomy waters, glowing in the dark with a luminous green-blue or white light. Some of these species travel and hunt in packs, following their prey to the surface at night, returning into the depths by day. Most of the world's smallest sharks live here. Pygmy and dwarf sharks no bigger than a cigar travel up and down the ocean for several kilometres each day. On the deep sea floor are such enormous sharks as the sixgill, sevengill and sleeper sharks. These eat the remains of food that sinks down from the sea's surface. Many deep sea sharks look primitive, but strangest of all are the frilled and horned goblin sharks. These look like the fossilized sharks that swam the seas 150 million years ago.

▲ LIVING FOSSIL

The frilled shark is the only shark shaped like an eel. It has six feathery gill slits, 300 tiny, three-pointed teeth and a large pair of eyes. Instead of a backbone, it has a firm, but flexible, rod of cartilage. These features tell us that the frilled shark resembles sharks that lived in the oceans millions of years ago.

▲ DEEP SEA JOURNEYS

The shortnose spurdog can be recognized by a spine at the front of each dorsal fin. It lives in large packs made up of thousands of sharks. It swims at depths of 800m in the northern waters of the Atlantic and Pacific oceans. Seasonally, the packs make a daily migration, from north to south and from coastal to deeper waters.

shortnose spurdog
(Squalus megalops)

▼ DEEPEST OF THE DEEP

The Portuguese dogfish holds the record for living in the deepest waters. One was caught 2,718m below the sea's surface. At this depth, the water temperature is no higher than a chilly 5–6°C.

Portuguese dogfish
(Centroscymnus coelolepis)

◄ SIXGILL SLITS

Most modern sharks have five gill slits, but primitive sharks, like bluntnose sixgill sharks (*Hexanchus griseus*), have more. These sharks are found at huge depths around the world. They have evolved (developed) slowly, and still have the features of sharks that lived millions of years ago.

▼ SEVENGILL SLITS

Broadnose sevengill sharks have seven gill slits. They have primitive, sharp teeth that look like tiny combs. They use these to slice up ratfish, small sharks and mackerel. Because some of their prey live near the surface, sevengill sharks travel to the sea's surface to hunt at night.

Broadnose sevengill shark
(*Notorynchus cepedianus*)

Did you know? Many deep-sea sharks have light-organs on their bodies.

velvet belly
(*Etmopterus spinax*)

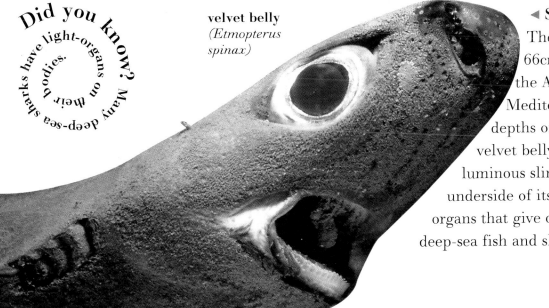

◄ SLIMY COAT

The velvet belly is 66cm long. It lives in the Atlantic and Mediterranean, at depths of 70–2,000m. The velvet belly is covered with luminous slime, and the underside of its body has special organs that give out light. It eats deep-sea fish and shrimps.

Freshwater Sharks

Although most sharks live in the salt water of the sea some, such as the bonnethead and sandbar sharks, swim to the mouths of rivers to give birth. There are a few sharks that swim all the way up rivers, and some swim into freshwater lakes. Atlantic sharpnose and spadenose sharks, and Ganges and Borneo river sharks swim in fresh water. Bull sharks are the species most often seen in fresh water. How this species' body copes with fresh water is not known. A fish that usually swims in salt water needs to find a way of coping with water that is not salt. On entering a river or lake, a fish used to salt water would be expected to absorb water and blow up like a balloon, but bull sharks do not. Somehow, they have found a way to keep the levels of salt in their blood low, so reducing water absorption in fresh water.

▲ **HOLY RIVER**
Shark attacks on pilgrims bathing in the holy Ganges River in India were once blamed on the Ganges river shark. Instead, they were probably made by the bull shark, which feeds on cremated bodies thrown into the river.

◄ **RIVER JOURNEYS**
Bull sharks have been seen in the Amazon, Congo and Mississippi rivers, and in other tropical rivers and lakes around the world. They gather at the river mouth, where edible rubbish is found during floods. Bull sharks are also sometimes called Zambezi sharks because they make regular journeys up Africa's Zambezi river.

Vishnu
In Hindu religion, the god Vishnu is believed to be the protector of the world. In legendary tales, Vishnu saved the sacred religious texts of India when the whole world was covered in water. This Indian picture shows him emerging from the mouth of a monstrous fish, probably a shark.

▲ KEYS SWIMMER
This bonnethead shark (*Sphyma tiburo*) lives near river mouths in the Florida Keys, in Florida Bay in the southeast of the USA.

▶ BORN-AGAIN SHARK
The Borneo river shark (*Glyphis*) was believed extinct until one was caught in 1997 by a fisherman in Sabah in South-east Asia. Until then, the only known specimen was 100 years old and displayed in an Austrian museum.

Borneo river shark
(Glyphis)

◀ LAKE NICARAGUA
Although they do not live all the time in Lake Nicaragua in Central America, bull sharks (*Carcharhinus leucas*) are also called Nicaragua sharks because they travel between the lake and the Caribbean Sea. It is thought that some female bull sharks swim to the lake in order to give birth to their pups.

231

Life on the Seabed

People once thought that all sharks died unless they kept swimming. This is not true. Many sharks that live close to the sea floor do so without moving for long periods of time. Wobbegong and angel sharks have flattened bodies that help them to lie close to the sea floor. Their skin colour also blends in with their background, hiding them from their prey as they lie in wait. These sharks take in water through a special spiracle (hole) behind their eye to stop their gills becoming clogged with sand. Some sharks that live on the sea floor, such as catsharks and carpet sharks, are not flattened. Whatever their shape, most are camouflaged with spots, stripes or a mottled pattern on their back.

▲ OCEAN CAMOUFLAGE
Sharks that live near the surface can also camouflage themselves. From above, the great white's dark back blends in with the ocean depths.

▼ SPOTTED ZEBRA
The adult zebra shark (*Stegostoma fasciatum*) has spots instead of zebra stripes. It has stripes on its skin as a pup. These break up into spots as the shark grows. It lives in the Indian and Pacific Oceans.

▲ AMBUSH EXPERT

The Pacific angel shark (*Squatina californica*) buries itself in the sand, and watches for prey. When a fish comes close, the shark rises up and engulfs the fish in its huge mouth. It then sinks back to the seabed, swallowing its food whole.

▲ CORAL COPYCAT

This tasselled wobbegong (*Eucrossorhinus dasypogon*) is invisible to its prey. It copies the colour of rock and coral, and has a fringe of tassels hanging down below its mouth that look like seaweed.

► SHELLFISH EATER

The leopard shark lives in the shallow waters of the Pacific, along the west coast of the USA. It swims slowly, searching the sea floor for the molluscs that it eats.

◄ JAGGED SNOUT

The common sawshark (*Pristiophorus cirratus*) has a long snout with tooth-like barbs along each side. Two sensitive barbels (bristles) hang beneath its snout. It mows through sand and seaweed on the seabed, catching its prey by slashing about with its barbed snout.

233

Prehistoric Seas

The first recognizable sharks lived in the sea 400 million years ago. These early sharks developed from primitive jawless fish. The golden age of the sharks did not take place for another 100 million years. Then, sharks of every shape and size filled the sea and ruled the oceans. They grew into both incredible hunters and giant filter feeders.

About 150 million years ago, all sharks of the golden age began to die out. They were replaced with new breeds of sharks, the ancestors of today's sharks. When the sea-going relatives of the dinosaurs became extinct, sea mammals (warm-blooded animals) began to evolve, and with them eventually arrived a gigantic predator – megalodon. This shark grew to 18m and is thought to be the ancestor of the great white shark. It fed on whales and dolphins, but eventually outgrew its food supply and it died out, too.

▲ CIRCULAR SAW

This strange spiral of fossilized teeth comes from the jaws of a whorl-tooth shark. This creature lived during the golden age of the sharks. Unlike modern species, this shark did not lose its teeth. Instead, they were rotated along its spiral system of teeth, then stored in a special chamber underneath the lower jaw.

▼ SCISSOR TOOTH

This is an artist's impression of the ancient whorl-tooth shark. This shark had a single row of sharp teeth in its lower jaw, and a scattering of broad, crushing teeth in the upper jaw.

whorl-tooth shark
(Helicoprion)

Did you know? Fossil sharks' teeth detected poison.

234

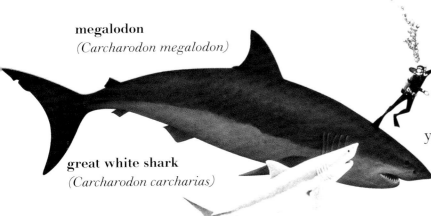

megalodon
(*Carcharodon megalodon*)

great white shark
(*Carcharodon carcharias*)

◄ MONSTER SHARK

Today's great white shark might seem a monster, but megalodon was three times bigger. It first appeared about 18 million years ago, disappearing two million years ago. It was the terror of the oceans.

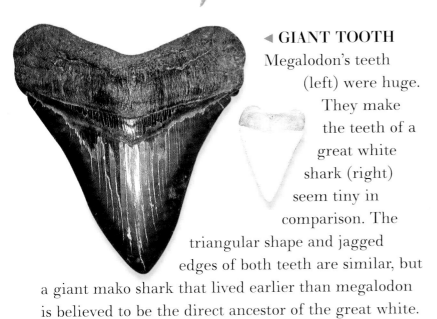

◄ GIANT TOOTH

Megalodon's teeth (left) were huge. They make the teeth of a great white shark (right) seem tiny in comparison. The triangular shape and jagged edges of both teeth are similar, but a giant mako shark that lived earlier than megalodon is believed to be the direct ancestor of the great white.

▲ RECONSTRUCTED JAWS

Fossilized teeth and some pieces of backbone are the only megalodon remains ever found. However, by using the great white as a model, scientists have been able to reconstruct its huge jaws. Over 2m wide, megalodon's jaws could have eaten several people in one big gulp.

► FOSSIL TEETH

These fossilized teeth belong to an ancestor of the salmon and porbeagle sharks. It lived about 40 million years ago.

► BIZARRE SHARK

This artist's impression of the spine-brush shark is based on fossils found in Glasgow. *Stethacanthus* is its scientific name. The shark has a strange spiny brush where its dorsal fin should be. No one knows what it is for.

spine-brush shark
(*Stethacanthus*)

Shark Relatives

Sharks have some close relatives. Skates and rays are especially similar to their shark cousins. Both have features that are found in sharks, including a cartilage skeleton, electrical sensors and skin teeth. In fact, skates and rays look like flattened sharks. They also come in all shapes and sizes, ranging from long guitarfish to giant manta rays. Like whale sharks, manta rays also filter plankton from the surface of the sea, but in a more unusual way. Turning somersaults in the water, the rays guide the plankton into their mouths with flattened horns at either side of their head. Another close relative of the shark is the ratfish. Looking like a cross between a shark and a bony fish, the ratfish is probably the long-lost descendant of mollusc-eating sharks that lived 300 million years ago.

▲ STING IN THE TAIL

One of 30 known species of sting ray, the southern sting ray (*Dasyatis americana*) moves through the water by rippling its broad pectoral fins. It uses its tail to dish out a barbed sting to any attacker.

▼ UNDERSEA RATS

Although they are relatives, ratfish look quite different from sharks. In fact, in some ways they resemble rats. They have a long, thin tail, smooth skin and rodent-like teeth. Male ratfish also have an extra, hooked clasper on their forehead, and use two pairs of claspers around their pelvic fins to grip the female.

ratfish
(*Hydrolagus colliei*)

▶ SHARK OR RAY?
The long, flat shovelnose guitarfish looks like a cross between a shark and a ray. Although it uses its tail to swim, it is more closely related to rays. It swims in the coastal waters of the eastern Pacific. An adult usually grows to 1.5m long.

shovelnose guitarfish
(Rhinobatus productus)

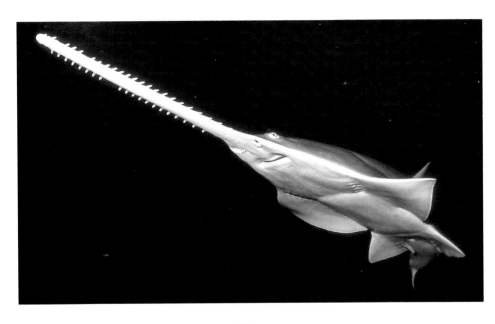

◀ SAW FISH
Saw fish (*Pristidae*) belong to the ray family. Unlike sawsharks, the pectoral fins of the saw fish grow forwards on its body, and are joined to the side of its head. Its gill openings are found on the underside of its head. It has a broad saw, which is lined with skin teeth that have been especially adapted for hunting.

electric ray
(Torpedo torpedo)

◀ ELECTRIC SHOCK
Torpedo, or electric, rays have special blocks of muscle in their wings that can produce electric shocks of up to 220 volts. They use this hidden weapon to knock out their prey. The shock can stun a human.

Did you know? Manta rays may grow to 7m across and weigh 1,400 kg.

▶ FLYING RAYS
Spotted eagle rays (*Aetobatus narinaria*) have broad pectoral fins which they flap like birds. The fins of some species span nearly 3m. Spotted eagle rays feed on shellfish and oysters, which they crush with their teeth.

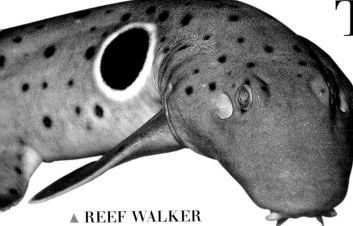

The Eight Families

Sharks fall into eight main orders (groups) divided according to different features. The most primitive order, including frilled and sevengill sharks, have more than five gill slits. Dogfish sharks have long, round bodies, and include luminous (glow in the dark) sharks that live in very deep water. The seven or more species of sawshark have a saw-like snout. Angel sharks look like rays and lie hidden on the seabed. Bullhead sharks have spines on both of their dorsal fins, and carpet sharks, like the wobbegong sharks, have short snouts and bristles on their snouts. Mackerel sharks, with their special, warm muscles, are awesome hunters. These sharks include the great white and mako. The ground sharks include the widest range of all, from catsharks to bull sharks, hammerheads, blue sharks and oceanic whitetips.

▲ REEF WALKER
Two pairs of muscular pectoral fins allow the epaulette shark (*Hemiscyllium ocellatum*) to walk over its tropical reef home. It feeds on the seabed of shallow waters around the Australian reefs.

▼ TYPES OF SHARKS
Modern sharks are divided into eight large family groups. These groups are divided into over 30 smaller families, and nearly 400 species. This number will probably rise as more species of shark are discovered.

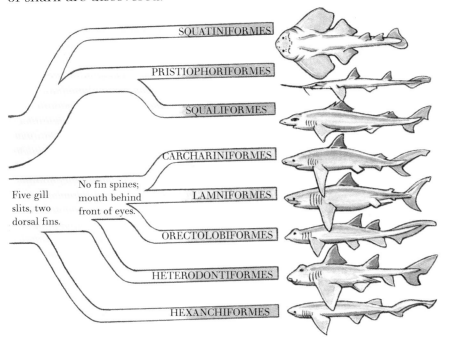

SQUATINIFORMES	Body flattened, raylike. Mouth in front.
PRISTIOPHORIFORMES	Snout elongated and sawlike. Mouth underneath.
SQUALIFORMES	Snout short, not sawlike.
CARCHARINIFORMES	Sliding flap that covers eyes.
LAMNIFORMES	No sliding flap over eyes.
ORECTOLOBIFORMES	Mouth well in front of eyes.
HETERODONTIFORMES	Dorsal fin spines.
HEXANCHIFORMES	Six or seven gill slits. One dorsal fin.

Five gill slits, two dorsal fins. No fin spines; mouth behind front of eyes.

◀ **PRIMITIVE SHARK**
The broadnose sevengill shark (*Notorynchus cepedianus*) is one of five species of primitive sharks. Each has six or seven gill slits. All swim in deep waters.

▲ **GROUND SHARK**
The swell shark (*Cephaloscyllium ventriosum*) is a ground shark. It blows up like a balloon by swallowing water and storing it in its stomach. When it is threatened, this amazing shark wedges itself firmly inside the cracks between rocks. It can be very difficult to remove.

Did you know? Pacific island children ride on nurse sharks' backs.

Food for the sharks
The Carib peoples buried the bodies of their dead relatives by ceremonially putting them into Lake Nicaragua in Central America. Many of the bodies were then eaten by bull sharks in the lake. One thief made a fortune by catching the sharks, slitting them open and removing jewels that had decorated the bodies of the dead. Until he was caught, that is ......

▶ **REQUIEM SHARK**
The sandbar, or brown, shark (*Carcharhinus plumbeus*) is a requiem shark, meaning 'ceremony for the dead'. All members of this family are active hunters. They rule tropical seas, hunting fish, squid and sea turtles. They are probably the most modern group of shark.

Friends and Enemies

No sharks spend all their time alone. They attract all kinds of hangers-on, including pilot fish, bait fish and a wide range of parasites, both inside their bodies and out! Sandtiger sharks are often seen surrounded by a cloud of baby bait fish. Too small for the shark to eat, the bait fish crowd around it for protection. Basking sharks are sometimes covered with sea lampreys, which clamp on to the shark's skin with their sucker-like mouths. To get rid of these pests, the giant sharks leap clear of the water and crash back down to dislodge them. Smaller parasites live inside each shark. These have adapted so well to life with sharks that they can only survive in one species, some in only one part of the shark's digestive system.

▲ STRIPED PILOTS

Tiny pilot fish often ride the bow wave in front of a shark's snout. Young golden trevally fish swim with whale sharks. When they are older and lose their stripes, they leave the shark and return to their reef homes.

▼ HITCHHIKER

A remora fish stays with a shark for most of its life. Its dorsal fin is designed like a sucker, which the fish uses to attach itself to the shark's belly. The fish then feeds on scraps from the shark's meal.

240

▶ SCRAPING CURE

Some fish use the shark's rough, sandpaper-like skin to remove their own parasites. Rainbow runner fish will rub against a whitetip reef shark's side. Behind one shark might be an entire group of fish lining up for a scrub.

◀ BARBER SHOP

Many sharks visit what scientists call cleaning stations. Here, small fish and shrimps remove dead skin and parasites from the shark's body, even entering the gills and mouth. This hammerhead shark is gliding past a cleaning station where several king angel fish have darted out to clean it.

▼ UNWELCOME FRIENDS

Strings of parasitic copepod eggs trail behind the dorsal fin of this shortfin mako shark. These parasites will have little effect on the shark's life, but if large numbers of parasites grow inside the shark, it can die.

▶ BLOOD SUCKER

A marine leech feeds by attaching itself to any part of the shark's skin and sucking its blood. Other parasites feed only on certain areas of the shark's body, like the gills, mouth and nasal openings.

Did you know? Pilot fish ride sharks' bow waves like dolphins on ships.

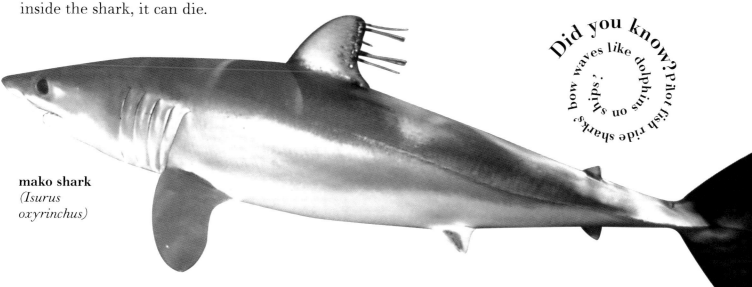

mako shark
(Isurus oxyrinchus)

Sharks and People

Sharks are feared because they attack people. However, only a few such attacks take place each year. People are more likely to be killed on the way to the beach than be killed by a shark in the water. Fortunately, attitudes are changing. Today, people have a healthy respect for sharks, rather than a fear of them. As we come to understand sharks, instead of killing them, people want to learn more about them. Diving with sharks, even such known threats as the great white shark or bull shark, is more accepted. People study sharks either from the safety of a cage or, increasingly, in the open sea without any protection. Such is our fascination with sharks that aquariums are being built all over the world. Here, more people will be able to learn about sharks at first hand, and not even get wet!

Jaws

The book and film Jaws *featured an enormous great white shark that terrorized a seaside town. The film drew great crowds and its story terrified people all over the world. It also harmed the reputation of sharks, encouraging people to see them as monsters, rather than the extraordinarily successful animals that they are.*

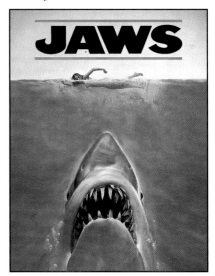

◀ **FEEDING TIME**

At tourist resorts in the tropics, divers can watch sharks being fed by hand. This activity is not always approved of. Sharks come to rely on this free handout, and may become aggressive if it stops. Inexperienced divers may also not know how to behave with sharks, resulting in accidents, although these are rare.

◄ ANTI-SHARK MEASURES

Anti-shark nets protect many popular South African and Australian beaches. Unfortunately, these nets not only catch sharks, like this tiger shark, but also other sea life, including dolphins and turtles. Less destructive ways of reducing people's fear of attack have yet to be invented.

► SHARK POD

Although a similar system is not yet available to bathers, one anti-shark invention seems to work for divers and, possibly, surfers, too. A shark pod can produce an electric field that interferes with the electrical sensors of a shark, encouraging the animal to keep its distance.

◄ SHARK ATTACK

Occasionally, sharks do attack. While diving in Australian waters, Rodney Fox was attacked by a great white shark. Rodney was possibly mistaken for a seal. He is probably alive because he did not have enough blubber on him to interest the shark and he was able to get away.

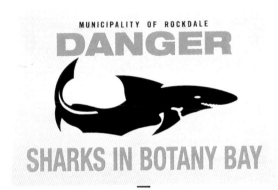

MUNICIPALITY OF ROCKDALE
DANGER
SHARKS IN BOTANY BAY

▲ SHARK WARNING

On many beaches, shark warning signs are used to tell people that sharks might be present. During the day, danger of attack is low, but it increases at night, when the sharks move inshore to feed.

243

Focus on the Great

The great white shark grows to over 6m long and is the largest hunting fish in the sea. Its powerful jaws can bite a full-grown elephant seal in half. Many people believe that the great white will attack people readily. This is not true. In the whole world, only about ten people a year are bitten by great whites. The shark does not eat these people. In fact it only bites them. Compared to the bites a great white can give, the bites it gives people are very small. Great white sharks are very aggressive, powerful fish and will only attack people if they think their territory is being invaded. The shark bites to say, "Keep away."

INTELLIGENT SHARK

The great white shows signs of 'intelligent' planning. It stakes out places off the Farallon Islands to the west of San Francisco, USA, where young elephant seals swim. In this way it avoids the large, possibly aggressive, adult bulls that could do it damage.

BODY PERFECT

The great white has the torpedo shape typical of a hunting shark. Its crescent-shaped tail, with its equal upper and lower parts, helps the shark to speed through the water. Although it is called the great white, it is not white all over, but grey on top and white underneath.

White Shark

GIANT SHARK ENCOUNTER

A great white shark dwarfs any diver. To a diver in a cage, it can sometimes seem that a shark is trying to attack. In reality, the shark's electrical sensors are probably confused. The diver's metal cage produces an electrical field in seawater – the shark is then likely to react to the cage as if it were prey.

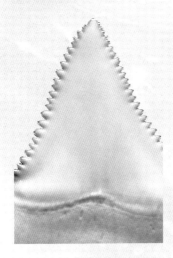

TERRIBLE JAWS

As a great white rises to take bait, its black eyes roll back into their protective sockets. Its jaws thrust forward, filled with rows of triangular teeth ready to take a bite. This incredible action takes place in little more than a second.

SHARP TEETH

The powerful, arrow-shaped teeth in the upper jaw of a great white have a serrated (jagged) edge. These teeth can slice through flesh, blubber and even bone. The shark saws through the tissue of its prey by shaking its head from side to side.

GAME FISH

To fishermen who hunt great whites for sport, the large breeding female sharks are the most attractive. The killing of these sharks has brought them near extinction in some places.

SHARKS

Conservation

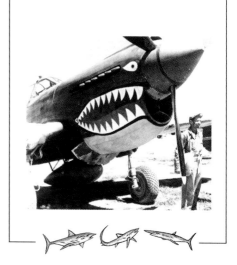

Flying Tigers

A Japanese god of storms is known as the shark man. In ancient Japanese legend, the shark man was terrifying. Encouraged by this fear of the shark, Allied airmen fighting the Japanese during World War II painted a tiger shark on their aircraft as a talisman. The pilots of these planes soon became known as "the flying tigers."

Sharks take a long time to grow to adulthood. They have very few offspring and may breed only every other year. Added to these factors, the hunting and killing of sharks can quickly reduce their numbers. This happened at Achill Island, on the Irish coast, where large numbers of basking sharks quickly disappeared, killed for their oil. Off the coasts of South Australia and South Africa, the great white shark was hunted as a trophy for many years. Numbers of great whites were so reduced that the hunting of them has since been banned internationally. A few countries control the fishing of sharks, to try to conserve (protect) them. However, in other countries, sharks are still hunted for shark fin soup, unusual medicines, and souvenirs. They are also sold to supermarkets as shark steak. Sharks, it seems, have more to fear from people than people have to fear from sharks.

◀ **WASTED SHARKS**
Each summer, many sharks are killed in fishing tournaments off the east coast of the USA. Sports fisherman are now learning to tag sharks, returning them to the sea alive instead of killing them. By tagging sharks, our understanding of shark biology is increased.

► **CRUEL TRADE**
Caught by fishermen, this whitetip reef shark has had its valuable fins removed. The shark was then thrown back into the sea, still alive. Without its fins, a shark is unable to move and, therefore, feed. It will quickly starve to death. This awful process, called finning, has been banned by some countries.

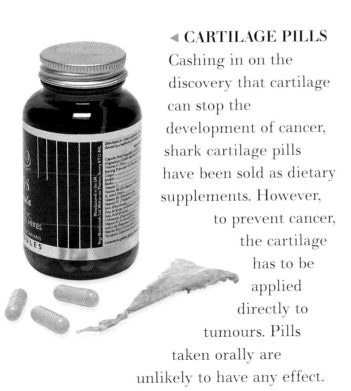

◄ **TRAVELLING INTO TROUBLE**
This tiger shark is being tagged to track its movements. Shark tagging programmes like this show that many sharks travelling great distances are being netted by several fisheries along their routes. Unless shark fishing is controlled internationally, far-travelling sharks will probably disappear from the sea altogether.

◄ **CARTILAGE PILLS**
Cashing in on the discovery that cartilage can stop the development of cancer, shark cartilage pills have been sold as dietary supplements. However, to prevent cancer, the cartilage has to be applied directly to tumours. Pills taken orally are unlikely to have any effect.

▲ **MULTIMILLION DOLLAR SOUP**
Shark fin soup is made from the dried fins of a shark. It has been prepared by chefs in oriental countries for over 2,000 years. The soup was once served to show favour to an honoured guest, and was also thought to be a health-giving food. Today, it is sold in cans and can be bought in supermarkets.

247

GLOSSARY

aestivation
A period of rest during heat and drought, similar to hibernation.

afterbirth
Any birth membranes and other tissues discarded or discharged into the sea when a baby shark is born.

albino
An animal that has no colour on all or part of its body but belongs to a species that is usually coloured.

anaconda
A type of boa.

antivenin
A substance made from the blood of mammals and/or snake venom that is used to treat snakebite.

bask
To lie for hours in the warmth of the sun, like a person who is sunbathing.

billabong
Branch of a river that comes to a dead end in a backwater or stagnant pool.

bioluminescence
The production of light by living organisms.

boas
A group of snakes that live in mainly North and South America.

brille
A transparent scale covering a snake's eye. It is also called a spectacle.

broadwing
A term used in falconry for birds with broad wings, such as buzzards.

camouflage
Colours or patterns on skin that allow animals to hide in their surroundings.

canine
A sharp, pointed tooth that grips and pierces the skin of prey.

cannibalism
Animals eating others of their own kind.

carcass
The dead body of an animal.

carrion
The flesh of dead animals.

cartilage
The strong but flexible material from which the skeletons of sharks and rays is made, rather than the bone found in most other animals with backbones.

catshark
The common name given to a group of sharks that are known in Britain as dogfish.

clasper
The male sexual organ in sharks consisting of two modified pelvic fins.

classification
Grouping of animals according to their similarities and differences in order to study them and suggest how they may have developed over time.

cloaca
Combined opening of the end of the gut, the reproductive system and the urinary system in reptiles, amphibians and birds.

clutch
The number of eggs laid by a female at one time.

cobras
Poisonous snakes in the elapid family, with short, fixed fangs at the front of the mouth.

cold-blooded
An animal whose temperature varies according to its surroundings.

colubrids
Mostly harmless snakes which make up the biggest group – nearly three-quarters of the world's snakes.

conservation
Protecting living things and helping them to survive in the future.

constrictor
A snake that kills by coiling its body tightly around its prey to suffocate it.

creance
A long line falconers use to train a bird before they let it fly free.

crocodilian
A member of the group of animals that includes crocodiles, alligators, caimans and gharials.

diaphragm
A sheet of muscle separating the chest cavity from the abdominal cavity, the movement of which helps with breathing.

diapsid
A type of skull with two openings on either side, behind the eye socket.

digestion
The process of absorbing food into the stomach and bowels.

digit
Finger or toe at the end of an animal's limb.

dinosaur
An extinct group of reptiles that lived from 245–65 million years ago.

diurnal
Active by day.

dominant animal
An animal that the other members of its group allow to take first place.

dorsal fin
The tall triangular fin on a shark's back. Some sharks have two dorsal fins, the front fin larger than the back one.

down
Fine, hairy feathers for warmth not flight. Young chicks have only down and no flight feathers.

ectotherm
A cold-blooded animal.

egg case
The leathery covering that protects a shark embryo developing outside its mother's body.

egg tooth
A temporary baby tooth on the snout of reptiles and the beak of birds that enables them to break out of their egg shells.

elapids
A group of poisonous snakes that includes the cobras, mambas and the coral snakes. Elapids live in hot countries.

electrical field
A zone surrounding an object, such as a muscle or nerve cell, that generates electricity.

embryo
The early stage of an animal before birth.

epidermis
The outer layer of the skin.

estuary
The mouth of a river.

facial disc
A circle of tiny feathers around the face of an owl.

falconry
Flying falcons or hawks as a sport. Also called hawking.

fang
A long, pointed tooth which may be used to deliver venom.

feeding frenzy
The name for what happens when sharks go berserk, slashing and biting anything that moves, when there is blood in the water or when they are presented with large quantities of food.

filter-feeder
Animals that sieve water for very small particles of food.

fingers
Feathers at the ends of a bird's wings, which bear a resemblance to human fingers.

fish ball
The ball that schools of fish make when attcked.

fledgling
A bird that is just beginning to fly.

gastroliths
Hard objects, such as stones, swallowed by crocodilians, that stay in the stomach to help crush food.

genus
A grouping of living things, smaller than a family, but larger than a species. The genus is the first word of the Latin name, e.g. in the King vulture's latin name *Sarcoramphus papa*, the genus is *Sarcoramphus.*

gestation
The period of time between conception and the birth of an animal.

gill arch
The part of the skeleton that supports the gills.

gill slit
The vertical openings on either side of the shark, just behind the head, from which the water taken in through the mouth and passed over the gills leaves its body.

gills
The organ by means of which aquatic animals, such as sharks, breathe.

gizzard
A muscular chamber in an animal's gut that grinds large lumps of food into small pieces or particles.

gut
The long tube in which food is digested and absorbed, running a winding path through an animal's body.

habitat
The kind of surroundings in which an animal usually lives.

harry
To intimidate another bird.

hibernation
A period of rest for certain animals during the winter, when body processes all slow down.

hybrid
In falconry, a hawk that is cross-bred – that is, its parents are of two different species, such as a saker and a peregrine falcon.

incubate
To sit on eggs to keep them warm so that baby animals will develop inside.

infrasounds
Very low sounds which humans cannot hear.

intestines
Part of an animal's gut where food is broken down and absorbed into the body.

invertebrate
An animal that does not have a backbone.

Jacobson's organ
Nerve pits in the roof of a snake's mouth into which the tongue places scent particles.

jawless fish
Primitive fish with sucker-like mouths rather than true jaws. They had their origins 500 million years ago and living descendants include lampreys and hagfish.

jess
In falconry, a leather strip that is fastened around a bird's leg, by which the bird is held.

juvenile
A young animal, before it grows into an adult.

keratin
A horny substance that makes up the scales of lizards, snakes and tuataras.

krill
Small shrimp-like creatures that swim in huge shoals. Krill form part of the diet of filter feeders such as whale sharks.

lift
The upward force acting on a bird's wings when it moves through the air. It supports the bird's weight.

ligament
A band of white, fibrous tissue that cannot stretch. It connects bones in a joint and strengthens them.

light organs
Special structures in a fish's skin that produce "cold" light, either by mixing particular chemicals together or with the help of luminous bacteria that do it for them.

longwing
A bird of the falcon family that has long, pointed wings.

lure
An imitation bird swung on a line to act as a target when training a falcon.

mammal
An animal with fur or hair and a backbone, that can control its own body temperature. Females feed their young on milk made in mammary glands.

manning
Making a hawk tame by getting it used to people.

mantling
Standing over a kill with wings spread to hide it.

mature
Developed enough to be capable of reproduction.

megalodon
A gigantic shark ancestor that first appeared 18 million years ago.

membrane
A thin film, skin or layer.

migration
Movement from place to place. Many birds of prey fly to warmer climates for the winter.

mobbing
When prey birds gang up against their predators and try to drive them away.

molar
A chewing and grinding tooth at the side of the jaw.

moulting
The process by which animals such as snakes shed their skin.

name
The same species (kind) of bird of prey often has a different common name in different countries. The bird called an osprey in Europe is often referred to as a fish hawk in North America. That is why birds are better identified by their scientific (Latin) name, which never alters.

nestling
A young bird before it has left the nest.

nictitating membrane
A third eyelid that can be passed over the eye to keep it clean or shield it.

nocturnal
Active by night. Owls are nocturnal birds of prey.

nutrients
Chemicals in food that, when digested, build blood, bone and tissue to maintain growth and strength.

order
A major grouping of animals, larger than a family.

ornithologist
A person who studies birds.

palate
The roof of the mouth. An extra or secondary bony palate that separates the mouth from the breathing passages.

parasite
An organism that lives on or in another living thing (its host), using the host as a source of food and shelter.

pectoral fins
The pair of large wing-like fins on either side of a shark's body.

pectorals
The powerful breast muscles of a bird, used in flight.

pellet
A ball of indigestible matter coughed up by birds of prey.

pelvic fins
The pair of small fins on the underside of a shark's body behind the pectoral fins.

pigment
Colouring matter.

pip
The first tiny hole a hatching chick makes in the eggshell.

piracy
When one bird harries another to make it let go of prey it has caught.

pits
Heat sensors located on either side of a snake's head.

placenta
A disc-shaped organ that is attached to the lining of the womb during pregnancy. It is through this that the embryo receives oxygen and nutrients.

plankton
Tiny aquatic organisms that drift with the water movements in the sea or in lakes.

plumage
The covering of feathers on a bird's body.

poaching
Capturing and/or killing animals illegally and selling them for commercial gain.

pod
A group of young crocodilians just out of their eggs.

predator
An animal that catches and kills
other animals for food.

prehistoric
Dating from the time
long ago, before people
kept records.

prey
An animal that is hunted and
eaten by other animals.

primitive
Keeping physical characteristics
that may have originated millions
of years ago.

pup
A young shark, particularly when
it has just been born.

pupil
The opening, which can be round
or slit-like, through which light
passes into the eye of an animal.

python
A group of snakes that lives
mainly in Australia, Africa and
Asia. Pythons have remains of
back legs and kill their prey by
constriction. They lay eggs.

rainforest
A tropical forest where it is hot
and wet all year round.

range
The maximum area in which an
animal roams.

raptor
Any bird of prey. From the Latin
rapere meaning to seize, grasp or
take by force.

rattlesnakes
Snakes that live mainly in the
south-west United States and
Mexico and have a warning rattle
made of empty tail sections at the
end of the tail.

receptor
A cell or part of a cell that is
designed to respond to a
particular stimulus such as
light, heat or smell.

regurgitate
Bring up food that has already
been swallowed

remora
A streamlined fish that attaches
itself to a shark's body with a
sucker, and accompanies its larger
companion everywhere.

reptile
A scaly, cold-blooded animal with
a backbone, including tortoises,
turtles, snakes, lizards
and crocodilians.

ringing
Attaching a small ring to the leg
of a bird.

saliva
A colourless liquid that is
produced by glands in the
mouth. Saliva helps to slide food
from the mouth to the throat.
In some animals, saliva also
aids digestion.

savanna
Regions of open grassland found
in places such as Africa.

scavenger
An animal that lives mainly on
the meat of dead animals.

scrape
A patch of ground cleared by a
bird to lay its eggs on.

scutes
The thick, sometimes bony,
scales that cover the bodies of
crocodilians and snakes.

sensory system
The collection of organs and
cells by which an animal is able
to receive messages from
its surroundings.

sexual dimorphism
The difference in size between
male and female birds, commonly
found among falcons.

shortwing
In falconry, a true hawk, with
short wings.

soaring
Gliding high in the air on
outstretched wings, riding on
air currents.

species
A group of animals that share similar characteristics and can breed successfully together. When naming animals scientifically, this is the basic unit of classification.

spiracle
A modified gill slit positioned behind the eye in sharks and rays.

spiral valve
A complicated folding of the tissues in the intestine of sharks that aids efficient digestion of nutrients.

spurs
Useless leg bones attached to the hip bones, which are found in boas and pythons and used during courtship displays.

stooping
When a falcon dives on its prey from on high at great speed, with wings nearly closed.

supraorbital bridge
A prominent ridge above the eyes in birds of prey, rather like an eyebrow.

swamp
A waterlogged area of land or forest, such as the mangrove swamps that are found in Florida, USA.

taiga
Forested parts of far northern regions of the world. Taiga lies just south of the tundra.

territory
An area of land that one or more animals defend against members of the same and other species.

thermal
A rising current of warm air, on which vultures and other birds of prey soar.

thermal corridor
A layer of water at a particular temperature.

threat display
The aggressive behaviour shown by some species of sharks when confronted by other sharks or sea creatures.

tooth whorl
A spiral arrangement of the teeth in some species of extinct sharks.

tropics
The hot regions or countries near the Equator and between the tropic of Cancer and the tropic of Capricorn.

tundra
The cold, treeless land in far northern regions of the world.

venom
Poisonous fluid produced in the glands of some snakes to kill their prey.

vertical migration
The daily movement that sharks make downwards into the deep sea by day and upwards to the surface waters at night.

vipers
A group of very poisonous snakes with fangs that fold. Some vipers have heat pits on their faces. Most vipers give birth to live young.

vocal cords
Two folds of skin in the throats of warm-blooded animals that vibrate and produce sound when air passes through them.

warm-blooded
An animal that can maintain its body at roughly the same warm temperature all the time.

warning colours
Bright colours that show others that an animal is poisonous. Bright colours also warn predators to keep away.

windpipe
In air-breathing animals, the breathing tube that leads from the mouth opening to the lungs.

wingspan
The distance across the wings, from one wing-tip to the other.

yolk
Food material rich in protein and fats, which nourishes a developing embryo inside an egg.

INDEX

Conservation Addresses

American Elasmobranch Society (USA)
http://www.elasmo.org

Audubon Institute and Audubon Societies (USA)
http://www.auduboninstitute.org
tel. (504) 861-5105

Born Free Foundation (UK)
http://www.bornfree.org.uk
3 Grove House, Foundry Lane, Horsham,
West Sussex, RH13 5PL, UK
tel. 01403 240170

Children's International Wildlife Sanctuary (USA)
http://www.ciws.org
P.O. Box 379, Saratoga, NY 12866-0379, USA

Greenpeace International
http://www.greenpeace.org
Keizersgracht 176, 1016 DW Amsterdam, The Netherlands
tel. 31 20 523 62 22

Royal Society for the Protection of Birds (UK)
http:www.rspb.co.uk The Lodge, Sandy, Bedfordshire, SG19 2DL, UK
tel. 01767 680551

Shark Trust (UK) http://ds.dial.pipex.com/sharktrust
36 Kingfisher Court, Hambridge Road, Newbury, Berkshire, RG14 5SJ, UK
tel. 01635 551150

Wildlife Conservation Society (USA) http://www.wcs.org
64th Street and 5th Avenue, New York, USA tel. (718) 220-5111

World Wildlife Fund (WWF International) http://www.wwf.org
Also WWF organizations in many countries including: Australia,
Austria, Belgium, Brazil, Canada, Denmark, Finland, France,
Germany, Greece, Hong Kong, India, Indonesia, Italy, Japan,
Malaysia, The Netherlands, New Zealand, Norway, Pakistan,
Philippines, Spain, Sweden, Switzerland, United
Kingdom and United States of America.

WWF-UK Panda House, Weyside Park, Godalming,
Surrey GU7 1XR, UK
tel. 01483 426 444

WWF-USA 1250 24th Street, NW., P.O. Box 97180,
Washington DC 20077-7180, USA
tel. 1-800-CALL-WWF